WHITE EYES, DARK AGES

DEBORAH RANDALL

White Eyes,
Dark Ages

BLOODAXE BOOKS

ISBN: 1 85224 222 1

First published 1993 by
Bloodaxe Books Ltd,
P.O. Box 1SN,
Newcastle upon Tyne NE99 1SN.

Bloodaxe Books Ltd acknowledges
the financial assistance of Northern Arts.

Cover printing by J. Thomson Colour Printers Ltd, Glasgow.

Printed in Great Britain by
Bell & Bain Limited, Glasgow, Scotland.

We were often at Brantwood all through the winter and I remember one morning when everything was white with snow, Ruskin's valet came to tell us that his master wished us to go into the drawing room before breakfast. This we did, and to our surprise found that all his Turner watercolour drawings were arranged on chairs in a kind of semi-circle, and other chairs had been put opposite to them so that we could sit down and look at them. There must have been quite a dozen drawings of the finest kind. The ground being covered with snow produced a beautiful white light in the drawing room, and the drawings had never looked so well before.

ARTHUR SEVERN
from his memoirs

Acknowledgements

My gratitude to Hawthornden and the Hawthornden Fellowship for providing not just a room of my own but a castle. And to Peter and Joyce who kept the home fires burning. And to my kitchen table.

The prose parts of this book (set in Bodoni type) are taken from the writings of John Ruskin, except for the quotation on page 12, which is by his father John James Ruskin, and that on page 58, taken from a letter to Ruskin by Rose La Touche. The poem 'Ever Your Rose' on page 58 uses lines from Ruskin's *Sesame and Lilies*. The other poems are all mine.

Contents

No good or lovely thing exists in this world
without its correspondent darkness.

The Demon Horse

I dream of semen
Unravelling from the lip and nostril
Of a phantom horse
A stallion
Well-hung
Who comes for me
Like a drum

And I run on the spot
Where trees have dropped
Their crockery
He's smashing plates
As he comes for me
His ectoplasm
Ghastly on the air.

I mean to mount him
But the reins
Are lashing like tongues
The back is bare
Treacherous black ice
The hair
A viperous frenzy.

Get me out of here
Before he mows me down
I am a man ethereal
Who quakes
Breaks into sweat
Makes in a dream
A two-backed seminal creature
I cannot ride.

Sun and Ice

We wait for each other at the white end of the world
Before the world was made and we could make it.

And the seal glides along the ceiling of ice,
His shadow true, through a curtain of water.

Water cast us on the wheel, water threw us together.

And I will make you red, will pierce the sun
To give you blood.

First the hood forced from your head
Then the plunge.

And I will turn the snow to hot hot milk
Shot from the nipple.

And I will kill your life-before-me,
Your origin in the wild wild sea.

I will softly close the hole
And blow a kiss.

Cuckoo

I am the cuckoo
I grow bigger
Uglier
On the portions of myself
You will allow
Or
The versions of yourselves
You think I am.

I am the bird
You borrowed from a child.

And the whole difference between a man of genius and other men, it has been said a thousand times, and most truly, is that the first remains in great part a child, seeing with the large eyes of children, in perpetual wonder, not conscious of much knowledge — conscious, rather, of infinite ignorance and yet infinite power.'

Jewel

I have darkness like the jewel knowledge,
And the beeches heed, the horseshoe bat
Sows up the last slit in the sky,
My treasure-toy turns on a spit of flesh,
Its facets sprinkle needles in the brain.

I have darkness like the jewel knowledge.

Around the shaved lawn runs a boy,
Refusing to come in,
His laughter plays crochet, this boy
Has run mad all night some say, but I say
This boy runs mad forever,
Through darkness, like the jewel knowledge
Flashing.

When a cat catches a bird it shatters feathers,
When a cat catches a bat
Darkness weeps,
The trees at the edge of darkness
Drip down their amber, ambling tears.

This boy refuses to come in.
Weep for him
But let him stay a child forever.
He is the jewel set against the dark.

'You may be doomed to enlighten a people by your wisdom.'
JOHN JAMES RUSKIN

We always suppose that we see what we only know, and have hardly any consciousness of the real aspect of the signs we have learned to interpret.

View from the Window

My house is my head
Behind my eyes where you believe I am dead,
Where you stand in my image blind,
Believing you see the same view from my window,
Behind my eyes, I live.

And you have smeared my glass coffin
In your search for borrowed beauty,
Believing you can wake me.

But I sleep, as I slept when I was old
With both eyes open,
Always fixed on the windows,
Waiting for mountains to fall
And the lake to catch them.

Try my slipper on your feet,
See if it fits,
Walk to the window and look
Where the lawns lap lazily,
And the lake is aflutter with butterflies,
Every one white and made of paper.

And if I put a small breeze over your shoulder
You shiver.

This man was clever
And only his shadow stands with you at the window.
The window shows the lake,
The lake shows a mountain already fallen.
Edifices crumble
Only to meet images of themselves.

Be quiet as you walk through my ribs,
Be humble.

I cannot but think it an evil sign of a people when their houses are built to last for one generation only.

Lightning Rend the House I Love

Lightning rend the house I love,
Rain return to every room,
Lacquer lust on ivy leaves,
Tip sleek leather.
For there is madness in the tomb,
Prepare each mortal and immortal thing
For ravening.

Wrath, the climax,
Wrath that flings the old, old song
From wall to wall,
For we with vengeance fought
Until the old piano wept,
Ting, ting,
Ting, ting, the rain.

Cherish me again to your dark core,
To the centre,
Tear me no more limb from limb
So cushions were my heart and liver,
Bell-pull, curtain-cords
My guts torn out.

Or then again the strings
That made me sing.
We were lovers.
No other would you have but him,
Chosen in the day
But darkness knows
Though you won't tell,
You kept the devil.

For Henry Acland

My friend,
My other bookend.

We prop a centre.
Read therein,
We loved, we loathed,
We liked.

That's friendship,
The truest, the best
Endeavour.

So
Until time's x-rays fail
We'll tell the tale.

Cat

Needs no explanation,
Swallows fire,
Strikes black water
Out of stone.

Serene,
Clean,
Tail a why, a whip,
A self-indulgent caress.

Has no needs,
Clever beyond creeds,
Spine sings ions onto finger.

Tooth and claw
Retract into night,
Sleep on the sword.

Needs no reason,
Lowlights make
Will o' the wisps,
Enticing the mind to empty.

Dog
(for Wisie)

Obedience owns this creature,
This creature owns contentment,
Has cracked life's perfect secret.

Named for wisdom,
Named for asking no question,
Telling no lie.

Whistler v. Ruskin

'Ruskin, you don't understand my art.
You are a woodworm found in stone,
To whom
Even the carved Colossus wouldn't yield
His passion.

You are an effigy, a sleeping knight,
With rectum made of stone, caught in the act.
And so,
You ponder how to make a fashion
Out of farts.'

On the Lake

This boat lulls...

Let them find me now
In the arms of electric eels.

The boatman slips the oars...

You are the devil's ferryman
Who takes them out and never returns them.

Into the water...

I deny it.

Easy as sending Moses...

I am the baby in the basket.

To his destiny...

It is better to conceive the sky as a blue dome than a dark cavity.

The Blue Dome

Summer is happening above the heads of the dead.
Her face is a raw daisy now
And the loom that is life has closed like the woven maypole.

Under her face, worms worming friendship,
Neighbour and neighbour mingle their benign bones,
Passing the time of day as they did aloft.

17

And summer if you are kind you shall forget me,
Smother her with a cypress tree which bears the load,
Hang the evening with bubbles from a blackbird.

In her coffin she hears the unnatural heat
Break into rain or the drumming feet of children
Playing over her pain.

Only then did she want air again
And water to burst on her skin pulping the parchment
Returning the spring to its source.

And summer if you are kind you shall disown
The black cavity behind the blue dome,
Summer if you are kind.

Cyanometer

The dream...
A machine
For measuring blue...

Bring me...
The sky
For a boy...

Who dreams
Of blue
Whose dreams...

Like blue
When bruised...
Turn black.

...throwing stones with Couttet, at the great icicles in the ravine...

Winterland

I shape my voice into a sphere
And cast it clean.
The game is the voice snowballing
Direct hits back.

Good to get rid of myself,
Throw stones in a glasshouse,
Knock out the ravine's white teeth.

This violence should be shocking
But this is exhilarating
White delinquency,
An arm lobbing a brain away.

I have hardly any real warmth of feeling, except for pictures and mountains...

Seeing Is Believing

My eyes have dissolved into a blue cravat.
What service did my eyes do me
When all is said and done?

And all is said and done
From looking long.
Shape and sign, signal and song,

Dissolve into what the mountain told me,
Nothing.
That last, that wildest, sweetest,
Nothing.

Glad Day

Take a boy.
Make a man.

He stands.

See mother.
The wilderness hasn't harmed me.

Though I spent forty days
And forty nights
In that place.

I've brought you samples
Chipped from those rocks.

Take. Eat.

This is my body.
This is my blood.
And still you tell me father
It isn't enough.

The next time you both come looking for me,
I shall deny you.

Mont Blanc

Standing at your shin
Looking up.

The giant-killer boy
Knew this thrill.

A moment slung between surrender
And his own power.

...the animation of a paralysed Christianity

Sunday's Child

They slaughtered me with the Sabbath.
It was no bloody thing
But a slow reckoning,
Repeated week by week.

I was made to contort my limbs
Into that day.
They pushed my head
Between my knees
Until I feinted.

The Earth in Fruit
(for Elizabeth Siddal)

Lamb with the burnished cords
Whose feminine imperative inspired
The eyes to smoke and oil to impersonate
Your beauty.

Nature put the earth in fruit,
Nature put your beauty there.

And you think beauty can save you.

I've seen your masters rub it out.

21

Art has you by the milky throat
And you have art enough to dote on death
As sacrifice.

And you think nature is beautiful.

And I made up my mind that this would never do. So after think-
ing a little more about it, I resolved that at any rate I would act
as if the Bible were true: that if it were not, at all events I should
be no worse off than I was before.

EFFIE

Flowers seem intended for the solace of ordinary people.

Primroses for Euphemia

When grass is lighted strongly by the sun
It is yellow and a blind man seeing yellow
In his first awakening thinks grass the same
As primroses or sulphur.

Likewise love is a trick of the light
A way of seeing not quite right
For there's no fusion in light's union
With flowers.

Smoking Out the Bees

As soon as you look away it happens,
The cell's division,
But they are indivisible,
The bees,
A double helix in search of a body,
An angry twist of ghost on a blue day.

And at their axis a Queen,
The female imperative upon which
Everything turns,
The constant centre, the rest crazy,
Because the seed is there,
The best-kept guarded secret.

She is the hot coal
Legacy to an ice age,
She hums under the set silence
Decreed and defied,
And when the bees are smoked out
She steals fire,
Takes it like a torch into the unknown.

The Water Nymph

And so I hope to love myself by loving you
The lure into the pool.

Draped by water, you and your sisters
Are in your element.

Fire, earth and air combine their strengths
To hold me back.

You disport in female liquors
Liquors that lubricate love
Get babies born.

But I'll not fall through a woman again.

It is of no use to trace the progress of alienation.

The Order of Release

Release all things,
Even take the life from them
That they may not be burdened
With a long life.

Go you snowballing girl
With him
Who rolled you.

I, the snowman,
I, the virgin
Who lay beside you
And left no trace in your bed.

Swimmers

The whirlpool takes up slack
Or her full skirt spinning up men
In motion,
And the mineral wall waits for my back.

Later the rain kept us in
And later I learnt the rain was lusting.
I liked him.

What is the cerebral vision
But a blind mole blundering?
Certainly words were wasted
In her presence
Where she screwed them scornfully
Like paper.

Her need for colour,
Wet and bright pulling her hair
Out of place.
He was a painter.
He plundered his box of colour.

Later they went to leap the river
Like two salmon aglitter.

I stayed in holding on to the table
Because it had begun to tilt
Under the weight of the flood.

All the words and sounds ever uttered, all the revelations of cloud and flame, or crystal, are utterly powerless. They cannot tell you, in the smallest point, what love means. Only the broken mirror can.

Foxglove

She has made a copulation by clairvoyance,
Made the dog fox come to take her,
Red man on white woman
He has her nature.

She stoops to stir the mirror
Then to break it.
She's cancelled daylight flowers
For phallic offerings.

Glenfinlas

Water shall always cleanse us of our differences.
Water in motion, water tumbling and tricking our vanities.
So we are children moulding water to our meaning.

Water

Shades of water,
Textures of water,
Colours of water.

Water to wine,
Walk on water.

My mirror is stilled water,
Stiff as the lake we walk in winter,
And a baby caught under.

That blue baby is myself,
But the glaze that is between us now,
The first thing we wore on our nakedness,
Now prevents our breath from getting through.

I cannot put my life back into him,
He is trapped by the very thing
That was warm and welcoming once.

Water has nothing to hide.
Water never meant to trap us.

Venice

Rank water throws up stones and their ripples
Endure the groaning centuries and the throwaway species
Man;
His splendour is soundless, only the rain spires
Striking the hour and big green bells
Beaten by effigy, and confetti of pigeon
Erode the silence and sigh of bridges.

My image follows in my footsteps, rats
Patter on the water, stones, and beauty;
And if I turn to find him, he
Is a pillar, and I am lonely for my brother
Changed by alchemy to this city's scrimshaw.

I looked for another world and found there is only this, and that
is past for me.

Search

I searched for a single man who didn't appear
Or come clean through cloud banks of countenances;
It was like contacting the dead who really were the living
And the awful realisation that you are he, the one not there.

An Enclosure on the Sea

My head is a cave
Flinging away light.
A cat's eye here
Would be extinguished.

My head is a nut
A germ arrested.
An engine humming
Underground.

My head is a shell
An enclosure on the sea
The lunacy
Of compressed ocean.

Haymakers

I'm growing my beard from the turret room
And very soon I'll climb down to youth and freedom
And cut me from the wizard who waits with wisdom
Peddling it in portions that can't restore potency.

So summer wasn't kind and didn't last forever
But it burns today and the gangers are about the fields
Embracing their light burdens
Like swatches of women in parody of the dance.

It's time to get everything in, lads to their loose lasses
Before the cannon in the sky fires a warning
And everything is over, the grains of sun snuffed out
As a smith would smother a red hot shoe in water.

One of the gangers a woman with a straight back
And every last thread of her hair up
How her demeanour mesmerises me
Because she slaves free, because she has no idea
That her labour becomes her.

B

Lucifer Lost

Because you are black
You came as a cat,
Because you are carnal,
You came as a beast.

Because you are forbidden,
I made myself naked,
Because you are taboo,
I wanted you.

But you came as a cat
And strung me with beads,
I flung you back
To velvet Hades.

Silk

And she who gave me birth
Used a silk purse.

There are women spinning
In Italy.

I imagine myself dismantled
By the sun

And their laughter and chatter.

I don't hear the cruelty in them.

I'm eating olives.
I seem to be eating my mother's ovaries.

The olive tree becomes her twisted arms.
I struggle.

They've exposed a fat grub
With an orifice for spewing silk.

I write to her today from Italy.
I tell her I am enjoying the sun.

I send silk love on a gilded page
And she doesn't suspect the cruelty in me.

By the Fire

Fire has filled me with red wine,
Using blood for woad
Has practised the ancient art
Of body painting.

Anointing the cadaver
Burning his name.

Vermilion vipers from the vine
Shake out their heads
And twine.

September has twisted her wings,
Collapsed into the dead trench between
Summer, winter.

Soot from the fire
Puffs on his knee
Recalling the unclean spore
From the penile toadstool.

He has heard the grave slam
The many small explosions of leaves
The last time he went to the wood.

And fire has brought him to consummation
Beginning the end.

JOAN

The Gardeners

Easy to love the garden and for the garden to give back
A blowsy affection.

We used to stretch full length along the path
And share passover with the bees.

The bees got fat on summer, they waxed their thighs.
You were already fat and melting in the summer heat.

We lay as if felled by flower or laughter
The absurd glory of that laughter.

Now you grieve and I waste, and you tell me, I wander
Down the same garden path.

These days I fall by accident and not design
But I still find you there
The same dear monstrous flower.

The Custodial Woman

She eclipses all flowers,
Her butcher's arms ready to hack
A meal into being,
Swill a putrid bowl in an aside,
Collect the cuckoo-spit from a sickman's mouth
As if it were pearls.

Her decent ugliness
Checks all beauty,
Even her strong wild hair
Is trussed,
Her head, a walking bust.

She turns duty into an art form,
Her love the rolled sleeve school,
No-nonsense artefacts surround her
And surrender.

Children pass through her,
She wears them awhile on her hip and breast
Maternal medals.
Her husband becomes her son
And she takes her son for a husband.
But her daughters.
Her daughters litter the house and sicken
Like jailed gypsies.

Butterflies Brought in by Her

Look in the face of a self-strung creature
For signs of the cat-gut tightening his cheekbone,
Turning his lip, down, down, and the cello-moan
For milk, for a stroke from a female hand.

The minerals clash with the plant-life,
The rotting guelder-roses in the bowl,
Posies nature gave and she arranged
To be near him, decomposing as he did.

His brain a fatal erosion, a rogue gene
Duelling with spirit, spirit the slippery elm
Crashing, wrenched from the black bridal bed,
A bouquet of stormy leaves tossed in the grave.

Summer lightning cutting the black cake
Every room had become, eyes put out
And an old fool playing for time
Gathering his daughters and calling them lovers.

They bury him in their blizzard of blossom,
His madness benign so they spoon him cream
Fill his lap for a moment, garland his neck,
Then flit away like confetti.

So she strokes and he forgives himself his fancy,
For collecting fossilised bread to feed the hungry
And hanging visions on his dimming walls,
For pronouncing no difference between a pinned and a free wing.

She had plucked and brought them in to be near him,
What had they been before she brought them in,
What were they now, the horror in that bowl
Of rotting butterflies, and worse than that,
The horror in her meaning.

Everything White, Everything Black

She plays or at least her hands do
And I feel china breaking in my heart,
It's good to see her workwoman's hands
Be beautiful for a change
Where they'd wring a chicken's neck,
Hoist linen sopping wet
Or cup dough into the oven,
They play.

They play, and then again they don't
She's playing with a fury
She's furious and her hands
Have become white rats,
Her tunes verminous
As they hurtle up and down the keys
Seeking escape.

And then she orders tea.
Tea comes orderly
Taken for granted like the next heartbeat.

But she has meddled with the black and white.

Above and Below

I walked to the crisp top,
A man and his own endeavour,
And it was up and up
Over heather.

And it was infernal, eternal
Winter,
Seizing fell, and river,
Lake and mountain.

The paralysis enabled us
To walk on water,
Hushed my footprints
As they passed.

It would not tell
I'd left the house
And you.

And you
Were in the house below
Filleting fish for dinner,
Fish with eyes like the lake
In winter.

Burning the Love Letters

She's arrested the words
So they can't fly
From her hands.

She is the witch-hunter,
The burner.

She keeps them for the fire.
Fire has a way with fancy
And with facts.

She sets them in
Their burning nest.
Fledglings fat
For cremation.

Just a job.
Just her conviction
They must burn.

She is
A comfortable woman
Unfit for the paper chase
When the burning birds
Get loose and flutter
Phoenix run amok
To taunt her.

...there is another sunshine, and that the purest, whose light is white, and its shadow scarlet.

Watching the Feeling

Why do you dress the naked light
Strangle the scarlet shadow as it spills?

Crimson is impure and sinful
But comes from white.

Nature has taken a fit
And murdered the sun.

O, my blue-remembered mountain
Swept to oblivion.

Why do you close the curtain?
Why did you pluck my sight?

...perfect rest which I have in your constant and simple regard.

She Sings

Joan sings
Her voice visits every room
Among the living and the dying
In the nursery and tomb.

I want somebody to be kind to me without making me think
– or feel...

His Favourite Seat

This rock-hewn seat in a favourite corner
Joins me at the hip,
And I sit and sit with it
Watching water fall
Until I can no longer tell
If I live.

The animated world goes on without me,
The mineral hours have closed my mind,
Heart still searching out its blood
And shunting round the hours,
Though clocks, even clocks,
Grow still and thoughtful.

This is a vigil of sorts,
To grow such a natural granite disguise
That it becomes me and I become the rock
With received wisdom,
To be a rock is to want for nothing,
No desire to save the world, myself,
Or even take another breath.
Not breathing, just sitting.

As I Entered the Great Cathedral

As I entered the great cathedral I became
Part of the floating population of the unborn,
I felt them rubbing shoulders
And the amniotic air was thick with us.

We swayed and swung, swung and swayed
In the great and gentle suspension
And the mother church played her great organ
And threw her ribs over our heads.

I choose this, sanctuary in her belly
Where the world comes filtering through
In colours distorted by waters, and I can't hear
How it is to go bare and unsupported.

As I entered the great cathedral
I sang and drank with fishes
And played cat's cradle with the bell-pull
Thinking it never would ring the changes.

Serpent in the Garden

The hottest days hurt most,
That cautery of sun through dust,
Striking at the sadness sleeping,
Practising a return to the womb,
Or tomb, but the stone is rolled away
And I must vacate the state where age
Rules somnolently, I am evicted
Down Eden's garden path
And it's all too lovely.

Too much bumping beauty in the blooms
Seeming pregnant with themselves,
If flowers give birth to flowers
And scent is a sea which swings
Against an old man's nose
As he rolls like a sailor ashore
And drunk and using his legs imperfectly
Slipping on the spilt nectar.

I can't even see for my brows
Have tangled into my eyes,
The ivy over windows and griefless dew
Hovers on lid and lip, I am newborn to drop
My moisture without manners
And so I totter on and this becomes
The first step and every living plant
A planet to be visited, I dive
To the centres, go under their sweet
Surfaces, break their small cache of waters.

How every bloom was nurtured then
And now they fend more free because
The gardener tends a rockery of red-hot
Poker, he who picked the cankerworm
Is less particular, and life eats life
In his garden.
Every Eden has a perimeter, the copper tree
By the kissing gate chinks tickets
On the heads of those who seek the wilderness.

Behind the gate the beech hangar
And a woodsman somewhere in the heart
Chopping at the arteries, it sounds a rhythm
Primitive and urgent on the lazy heat
Eating out an appetite to use his sinews
And I am drawn to watch this lion flaunt
Vitality, to voyeur what I never had,
Through the gate of no return,
No kiss to remember, my loose hide
Catches on a splinter, I slip out of it.

Over my head in the lime tree
A bees' nest disturbed, nature's acoustic dust
Dancing, and I hurry by thinking of felled lions,
Out of the strong came sweetness,
Nature's taxidermy which animates the dead
By thousands, everything run wild
Made by a careful whim, tossed in an aside
Into being, even the serpent condemned
To crawl on his belly, under the heel.

Dear creator, I have stepped on an adder,
Have met the serpent on the highway
Seeking admission to Eden, under my heel
The oldest sin in nature and I revile him
Automatically, the accusation is let out
And amok in the woods before I can call it back
And control the horror that squirms
From bowel to mouth, as if I had fed on worms,
Trusted the serpent to conceal its identity
To the end of time.

The warrior woodsman comes like a bored satyr
To dispose for pleasure, the day is otherwise
Too dull and this a diversion, he strikes
And I see the creature was only just
Unravelling sleep and sun, had no evil intention,
And strikes again so the serpent shall not enter
The garden, it embraces the weapon,
Binds the weapon up to the hilt, springs coils
Like a running weed and won't be shaken.

He must kill it by ingenuity, by scraping
And striking, scraping and striking, as if
He were kindling a fire from scratch but this death
Is many, and the muscle must be severed
To disown the head, which staved in, falls from grace
And lies like a leaf agape with disbelief,
Then he swings the thing over his head
Into time and space, a girl letting out her hair
Could not be more casual.
And that was a prelude to madness.
I tumbled from innocence, knocking into
Every flower as I went back, afraid to look
In their heads anymore, because baby serpents hatched within.

Maydance

Schoolgirls tug and toss on the washing line
Throttling a pole as they close the tourniquet
And a wheezy organ continually resuscitated
Breathes heavily like lust-in-dotage
Urging the virgins to fecundity.

ROSE

The Kiss

This innocence is more assumed than real
For we have passed the kiss between us
Like original sin writ loud and hot
On her girlish cheek.

It is my lot to live estranged
From the man inside
He has judged himself
And found himself wanting.

He walks in the image of another
And lesser being
Carrying her kiss until
It burns a hole in him.

And girl, I'm glad we've kissed,
Glad it was out of doors
Where the flowers have vulvas
And bees crawl in.

Do I want to keep her from growing up? Of course I do.

Need

My need for her became necrophilia.

I truly wanted her dead
But could only induce sleep.

Even from sleep she cried out like a woman
Wanting a lover.

St Crumpet

Patron saint to children.
Butter him up.
Fill his empty honeycombs
With sweet resin.
Mine his waxy surfaces
Relish his soft centre.
Make him drip.
Suck him.
Squeeze him.
Kiss him.
Tease him.
Let his ghee
Run down your chin.
King of the golden river.

Catch as Catch Can

This concerns no one
Especially no man.
Catch as catch can.
Lay no hand
Upon her shoulder.

Nor check the bud
Which didn't grow
Nor wanted to.

Catch as catch can.
The water thrust
Through her hands,
And the light did too.

Sister to an amaryllis,
Belladonna lily knew.
This concerns no one,
Especially no man.

...the conditions of my life (which I cannot alter) do not make it possible to be well and happy.

... I could tell that I care for him very much now, with my child – or woman heart.

His Letter

She kept his unread letter pinned under her breast.
And when it hatched, and scratched,
She took no notice.

His words were fledglings and she had the power
To feed them or to dash them.

She chose, or made no choice, it happened
They fell on stony ground and squirmed

Like worms or the soul of man, exposed.

Her Letter

He keeps her between two slices of gold,
A sandwich
Totally inedible.

Ophelia Drowning

Come back into the stream,
Lie among the morphine and the dream,
Seal the shadows to your breast
Then rest,
Sweet troubled girl.

Go down beneath the lilies' kindly hands
For they shall take the fire from off your brow,
And waters quench you;
Sleep among the herbs and minnow.

No more tears.
The heron sups your eyes
And flies with angels.

I can't let her go on lecturing me as if she were the Archangel
Michael and the Blessed Virgin in one – because flesh and blood
won't stand it.

The Snow

We're creatures of a hothouse,
She especially,
Maiden ferns loll out their tongues
To lick her beads of dogma,
Ambergris oozed from her fervid imagination.

A girl with the mad rolling eyes of a saint
Looking for heaven.

She found Satan.
She finds Satan in me,
A dark coil ready to spring
And she uncertain whether to court or cure me.

We talk across the room
Without words.

Her tremulous fear
Twists her into a wraith.

She pulls prayers out of the air
Collects them like useless feathers.

Satan flew up like Icarus
And she cherishes his fallen feathers.

The snow is the dust from his glory.
She stuffs a pillow with his sins,
Sleeps herself into
A righteous corpse.

'I wonder if you remember me at all' – ROSE LA TOUCHE

Ever Your Rose

You cannot hammer a girl
Into anything.
She grows as a flower does,
She will wither without sun;
She will decay in her sheath,
As a narcissus will,
If you do not give her
Air enough;
She may fall,
And defile her head in dust,

If you leave her without help
At some moments of her life.

But you cannot fetter her;
She must take her own
Fair form and way
If she take any.

Kate Greenaway

She thinks she can crack admittance
Through my glacial film.
She thinks nothing moves in me
But senility.

But my eyes slither
To take in
That she herself is not young
Or pretty.

She sees something in me.

I see her children.
Little girls in petals.
I slip them onto my knee.
That's all I need of Kate Greenaway.

The Ice House

Dark ages wear white eyes,
I want her
Who disturbed me like ice and fire.

A roundhouse surrounds a sad spell.
The sorrow is palpable,
It freezes doves in their tracks.

This was our dovecote,
A keep for the parts of us too tender
To venture in the world.

I stand at the centre
As the drum revolves
Her song from the heart's chamber.

We were born dead.
We might as well live
To mine the ice from our eyes.

Turneresque

Throw open all the windows then
Where genius painted glass
And mortals may walk through
Without receiving
A shard to the heart.

The dainty white glove
Has arrested the organ
And doves dip their wings
Strike out at canvass.

Down fuels us
And then the angels
Who touch men
Make them mad.

Or yearn for the moment
Between contraction
And expulsion
When the feathers weep.

Drop beauty on the cataract
Restore vision so
The eye shall
Move the heart.

You Do Not Know My Life

The abomination is, to have made this woman from her image.
How my eyes herded her three times a week for years.
For years she brought my watercress and letters
And only here and now I ponder
Because the snow has pinched her tattered cheeks
And sucked the ancient blood she needed
To get her up the lane in winter,
How she had to tread cut glass to water,
Spoke to me from duty, never pleasure.

Here is the old woman who brings my watercress and letters
Three times a week, three miles through sun or snow
Invisible and unremarked for years.

The shepherdess, her lambs long gone for slaughter.
No complaint on her cracked lips which are a wound
Wearing salt, the things she could say and doesn't.

My salads sprout out of her fist and she transfers them
Tenderly,
She struggles home in sackcloth,
I watch her crook the snow by the neck, unpile it
From her path.

And then I don't think of her again.
But she brought to mind a waterfall once seen
Falling upwards by force of unnatural weather.
It peeled off in violent geysers of rainbow hue
Defying every assumption of how, and where,
Water should fall.

Snowdrop

He sentenced me to be a man.
I searched for a man
But found a flower.

He wanted me to be a boy.
I wanted to be a girl.

He made my life a misery
Until

I acquired genius beyond gender.

But I wanted him dead.
I wanted him planted in the ground.

I was innocent.
Now I am old.
Now I am innocent again.

And he is planted in the ground
Like a flower.

I pardon him.
He pardons me with a drop of snow.

We weren't sons or fathers,
Girls or flowers.
It doesn't matter.

Bitter Red

The decades steep in red.
Icicles bleed.

The garden waits
After the eviction.

Stalactite meets stalagmite
While waiting.

Time has no saviour.
The garden gives over.

I seem born to conceive what I cannot execute, recommend what I cannot obtain, and mourn what I cannot have.

A Winter's Ride

We force belief
Because belief won't come of its own accord.

Air stiff as a board today.

We walk, don't talk
In the wood.

The wood slips out of its clothes.

You run ahead then back over my shoulder
Leaving your tendrils to tickle.

Stag-beetles in rut,
Why should there be fear in that?

But there was.
They made the spring hideous.

Another season swapped for winter.

Your little dog is quite a man,
A ticklish muff you love to love.

I go barking round the bend.

Think me mad
To hear the cuckoo in December.

Hiccuping a warning.
Don't be a fool.

But demon hooves are coming for me.
I hear the crazy pattern of minced ice

And powdered leaf.

My Alice, you shrink.
Did we hope to save ourselves by alchemy?

Give me your hand to swing
In and out of the blighted air.

Give me your hair for reins.

Fragments of rose
Scattered on marble.

In the spark of your heel
I am unstruck tinder.

You rattle your relics.
You have stripped me to the bone.

In winter we walk on water
Talk through gauze.

A gelding has nothing more to lose.
I draw a veil on the rest.

Let white be our trysting colour then,
And we the ghosts who'll meet again

And have our way
In time.

How to Get Your
Product to
Market

A guide to design, manufacturing,
marketing and selling

by Louise Guinda

HARRIMAN HOUSE LTD
3A Penns Road
Petersfield
Hampshire
GU32 2EW
GREAT BRITAIN

Tel: +44 (0)1730 233870
Email: enquiries@harriman-house.com
Website: www.harriman-house.com

First published in Great Britain in 2014
Copyright © Harriman House 2014

The right of Louise Guinda to be identified as Author has been asserted in accordance with the Copyright, Design and Patents Act 1988.

ISBN: 978-1-908003-63-8

British Library Cataloguing in Publication Data
A CIP catalogue record for this book can be obtained from the British Library.

 Harriman House

This book is dedicated to my dad Frank Carr, the original productpreneur, and son Ali Guinda, hopefully a future productpreneur.

FREE EBOOK VERSION

As a buyer of the print book of *How to Get Your Product to Market* you can now download the eBook version free of charge to read on an eBook reader, your smartphone or your computer. Simply go to:

http://ebooks.harriman-house.com/producttomarket

or point your smartphone at the QRC below.

You can then register and download your free eBook.

FOLLOW US, LIKE US, EMAIL US

@HarrimanHouse
www.linkedin.com/company/harriman-house
www.facebook.com/harrimanhouse
contact@harriman-house.com

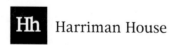

Contents

About the author

LOUISE GUINDA HAS SUCCESSFULLY brought two products to market: the Cot Wrap, a breathable alternative to cot bumpers; and Safebreathe Hoppy and Patch, breathable soft toys. Safebreathe Hoppy and Patch were snapped up by high street chain JoJo Maman Bébé from launch and the Cot Wrap is the best selling cot bumper on **Amazon.co.uk.**

Before founding her business Safe Dreams (**www.safedreams.co.uk**), Louise worked as an auditor for a 'Big Four' accountancy firm. Although this background was good preparation for the financial side of running a business, Louise had no experience of product design, manufacturing, marketing or selling. It took her two years to teach herself these skills, learning as she went along. It is for this reason that Louise decided to write *How to Get Your Product to Market* – to help speed up the process for others following in her footsteps.

Connect with Louise:

@productpreneur
www.facebook.com/productpreneur
louise@productpreneur.co.uk
www.productpreneur.co.uk

Acknowledgements

SPECIAL THANKS TO the following successful productpreneurs who gave their time to help with this book:

- Patrick Mathews of Breffo (**www.breffo.com**)
- Rena Nathanson of Bananagrams (**www.bananagrams.com**)
- Claire Mitchell of Chillipeeps (**www.chillipeeps.com**)
- Marc Ward of Jamm Products (**www.jammproducts.com**)

Thanks also to Clare Yarwood-White, Keira O'Mara of Mama Designs, Lara Milanova of Hamster Bags and Cara Sayer of Snoozeshade.

The Safe Dreams story: from a near-tragedy to a successful business

If I can do it, anyone can.

I AM LIVING PROOF that anyone can become a successful *productpreneur*. If you are wondering what I mean by that, here is a definition:

> *Productpreneur: A person who invents, creates or designs a product and brings it to market in the hope of making a profit.*

As a chartered accountant I may have had a head start in knowing how to run the financial side of a business, but these skills are not crucial for a business owner; most of the financial knowledge you will need can be picked up from books or easily outsourced to a professional. The hard and time-consuming part of running a business is designing your product, finding someone to make it, making sure it is safe, and finally marketing and selling it.

I had no knowledge of these things, so I was starting from square one. Although I have always been very risk-averse and lacking in confidence, I hated being an auditor and this gave me the determination to take the leap into running my own business.

What kind of business should I start?

I came up with lots of ideas – bookkeeping, opening a café, contract cleaning of offices – but in the end it was a near-tragedy which occurred when I was a new mum on maternity leave which led to my light-bulb moment.

My son Ali, like most babies, loved to snuggle into anything soft, including the cot bumper which lined his cot. I bought the bumper along with matching bedding before he was born. As the shops were full of bumpers, I hadn't thought twice about their safety. However, one day I came out of the shower and found Ali with his face completely submerged into his cot bumper. His face had turned a funny shade of blue and he was clearly not getting enough oxygen.

I thanked my lucky stars that I had checked on him when I did and immediately pulled off the cot bumper and threw it away. This wasn't the end of the problem though, because after this Ali would be constantly waking up in the night with an arm or leg stuck between the cot bars, or having lost his dummy through the gaps. The solution to this problem was clear to me – I needed a safe cot bumper that Ali would be able to breathe through.

I had spotted a gap in the market.

I searched for a breathable yet padded fabric and discovered Airmesh, which is often used in sports products and was starting to be used more widely in baby mattresses. I found that breathable cot bumpers made from Airmesh have been around for years in the US but, puzzlingly, they weren't available in the UK. I paid a fortune to have one shipped over but it was worth it, as it completely solved my problem.

The easiest option, of course, would have been to become a UK distributor for the American mesh cot bumper brand. However, although it was safe, the mesh bumper was ugly. It was made from scratchy polyester mesh with a shiny satin-like border, and I felt that it was not suited to the UK market, as our preferences are generally more towards natural fibres, such as cotton.

I wasn't interested in selling a product which was so unattractive, as parents would only buy it as a last resort if, like me, they weren't getting any sleep. I wanted a product that was pretty, which parents would be happy to use from Day 1.

There, I said it.

I didn't invent a totally new product from scratch; I tweaked an existing product to make it more suited to a new market. What I did invent was a new mesh-hybrid with an inner surface of 100% cotton

(Safebreathe fabric). I also replaced the scratchy satin edging with a soft natural cotton fabric.

Why had no one else thought of this idea?

The question of why no one had done this before held me back by about six months. There was clearly a market for breathable cot bumpers in the UK as when I posted about being woken up during the night because of trapped arms/lost dummies on parenting forums, plenty of other parents were having the same problem. Some were taking extreme measures like putting cardboard on the inside of their child's cot.

As I had so much to learn, it took 18 months from first having the idea to the moment when my Cot Wrap finally hit the market. It was featured in a catalogue with a huge circulation, so sales pretty much took off right away and it was a struggle to get enough stock made in time to keep up with the demand.

Now, the Cot Wrap outsells all other cot bumpers on **Amazon.co.uk** and is exported to eight countries around Europe. However, frustratingly, although it is carried by lots of little high street stores around the country, I have never managed to get it into a big store. As we have six colours and two styles (12 product lines in total – too much for any store to carry), it is much more suited to being a specialist internet product.

I didn't achieve my goal of getting into a large retailer until I launched my second range of products, Safebreathe toys, which are made from the same Safebreathe cotton fabric as the Cot Wrap. The toys were stocked by the high street chain JoJo Maman Bébé from launch.

It hasn't been easy.

I've made many mistakes which I am not afraid to share. During the six months when I was too scared to do anything about my idea, a competitor from Australia launched in the UK – their product is more like the American polyester mesh cot bumper, which means it is much cheaper than Safebreathe fabric as cotton is very pricey. There was a worldwide cotton crisis during the year I launched that meant that I had to raise my prices. I've had various quality issues, have struggled with cash flow and nearly gone out of business a few times. I've also had many bizarre experiences, like being featured on the BBC website when the launch of the Cot Wrap was delayed because of the chaos caused by the volcanic ash cloud in 2010, and trying to do a pitch on live TV with a crying baby in my arms.

This book will give you a step-by-step guide of how to turn your great idea into a reality. I will tell you how to be sure that there is a market for your product before investing too much of your time and money. I will explain the basics of how to protect your product through patents, design registration and trademarks, and, probably more importantly, how to make sure that you are not infringing on anyone else's intellectual property.

We will look at how to create a brand which your customers will trust, how to make those customers aware that your product exists and, finally, how to contact and grab the attention of retail buyers.

Introduction

SO YOU HAVE COME up with an idea for a new product that you are sure could be the next big thing. Maybe you have invented something groundbreaking that will make people's lives easier, or simply tweaked an existing product to make it better.

Maybe you consider yourself to be more of a designer than an inventor and you are sure that your creations would be a huge hit on the high street. You could be exactly right – there is currently a big trend towards high-quality, UK-designed products and major retailers, such as John Lewis and Liberty, are snapping up products from craft sites like Etsy (**www.etsy.com**) and Folksy (**www.folksy.com**).

You are probably wondering why your fantastic product idea isn't already out there. Somebody may well have come up with the idea before but perhaps they had neither the skills nor inclination to do anything about it and just got on with their daily life.

By reading this book you are proving that you are different. You are one of the few people who has both an inventor's mind *and* an entrepreneurial spirit; a combination that is necessary for success.

Creative people tend to have lots of different ideas. If that's you, remember what your mother told you about having your fingers in too many pies. Flitting from one idea to another and failing to truly focus on one single idea may ruin your chances of success. Choose your best idea, research it fully, then make a decision on whether it is viable. If it is not, then and only then move on to the next idea.

There are six steps involved in making your idea a reality:

1. Make sure there is a market for your idea.

2. Protect your idea so no one can copy you.

3. Create a prototype and find a manufacturer.

4. Raise cash and start your business.

5. Create a brand and shout as loud as you can.

6. Grab the attention of high street buyers and get your product on the shelves.

I will look at these in turn below.

1. Make sure there is a market for your idea

Finding products similar to your idea already out there is not necessarily a bad thing. Most successful ideas come from tweaking an existing product to make it better. This is what many successful entrepreneurs of our time have done: James Dyson didn't invent the vacuum cleaner and Christian Louboutin wasn't the first to make the soles of a shoe red. Dyson made a slick vacuum cleaner which didn't require messy dust bags, while Louboutin's red soles have become a fashion statement.

If there are similar products already on sale this is proof that there is a market for your product. This will make marketing much easier, as you won't have to educate people about why they need your product. They will already know. You just need to make sure that there is room for your product in the market: your twist must be so amazing that people will be willing to take a risk on something that is new to them – something they have not tried before.

Is your twist good enough? Chapter 1 will show you how to do market research to make sure.

If there are no similar products available, you have to either come up with a genius idea that potentially could make you a lot of money, or there may be a good reason why no similar products exist – perhaps that nobody wants to buy such a thing. In order to find out, you need to do your market research really thoroughly. Again, Chapter 1 will show you how.

2. Protect your idea so no one can copy you

Even if your idea is a twist on an existing product, you don't want to spend money creating and marketing it, just to find that someone else has copied that twist.

The main ways in which you can prevent someone from copying your idea, or your intellectual property as we call it in this context, are through patents, design rights/registration, trademarks and copyright. Chapter 2 will explain each of these in more detail. In most cases, having some form of protection will deter potential copiers.

Equally important is to make sure you won't be infringing someone else's intellectual property by selling your product. Chapter 2 explains how you can do this without spending a penny (or very little).

3. Create a prototype and find a manufacturer

If your product is not something which can be produced on a small scale, a prototype is essential to demonstrate your product to potential retailers and manufacturers and to get their feedback before you invest money in mass production.

Sometimes creating a prototype can be very easy – for example, if your product is sewn and the fabric is widely available, all it will involve is getting out your sewing machine or finding a local tailor or seamstress.

If your product is more technical, creating a prototype will require outside help. You may even need to raise money beforehand to pay for the prototype and tooling. If this is the case, it is incredibly important that you have done your market research and protected your IP beforehand to make sure you are not wasting your money and that you can't be copied.

The good news for those with ideas for more complex products is that once you have a prototype and tooling, it may be viable to mass-produce your product in the UK, which will make life a lot easier. For sewn products and anything else which is very labour-intensive, unless you are able to sell your product for a high price point, you may find that you have to produce it in a country with lower labour costs.

Chapter 3 will give you the information you need on these areas.

4. Raise cash and start your business

Finding the money to get to the point of making your first sale can be the hardest part of all.

Starting a business is like running an old car; costs that you would have never anticipated seem to spring up all the time. So work out how much you think you will need and double it (or even treble it).

If you don't have a lot of savings or generous family and friends, raising finance can take a lot of time and energy. You will need to write a business plan in order to convince lenders or investors that your business will make money.

Head to Chapter 4 to find out more.

5. Create a brand and shout as loud as you can

You could have the most amazing product in the world, but if it is presented shoddily people won't trust it. And if they don't hear about it in the first place, obviously they won't be able to buy it.

Good branding will lead customers to trust your product and make them feel like they just have to buy it. Branding is an area where you need to invest time and money. Your logo, website and packaging should reflect just how amazing your product is.

These days it is simpler than ever to get the word out about your product through social media. The internet, and especially Twitter, have made journalists much easier to get hold of, so getting into newspapers and magazines isn't as difficult as it once was and doesn't require you to hire an expensive public relations agency.

Chapter 5 will give you ideas on creating a strong brand and how to market your product.

6. Grab the attention of retail buyers and get your product on the shelves

There is no harm in contacting potential buyers as early as possible (once you have protected your idea) to get their feedback. Retailers are always keen to find the next big thing before their competitors do. They are used to seeing unfinished products which are the wrong colour, or for which the packaging hasn't been finalised. Buyers usually have a very good idea of what will sell in their stores – it's their job to get this right, after all – so approaching them can be the most valuable form of market research.

However, buyers are notoriously difficult to get hold of. They are constantly approached by would-be suppliers and receive emails about new products on a daily basis – buyers don't have the time to reply to every email they receive. Your chances of being taken seriously are much greater if you have your branding taken care of and can convince them that your business is big enough and experienced enough to be able to fulfil their orders on time.

Head over to Chapter 6 to find out how to grab the attention of buyers.

***

Transforming your idea from a dream in your head into an actual product on the store shelves is not easy (if it was, everyone would be doing it), but it is certainly possible. I am living proof: I have launched two successful products – the Cot Wrap and Safebreathe toys – despite having no relevant past experience.

Since starting a business, I've become a Jill-of-all-trades – I've learned about web programming, graphic design, photography, fabric, sewing techniques – I've even written a book!

If I can do it, you can too.

CHAPTER 1

Make Sure There Is A Market For Your Idea

DRAGONS' DEN HAS MADE a sport out of humiliating would-be entrepreneurs who are convinced that their idea is just what the world has been waiting for. If only the poor fools had done their homework beforehand – if only they had asked impartial people who represent their target market what they thought about their product rather than just their family and friends, they would have saved themselves from embarrassment on national TV.

This chapter looks at how to assess whether your idea is worth pursuing and conduct market research – an essential step before you go any further.

Is your idea original?

Inventions usually arise out of a problem for which there is no solution available. The world changes fast, so new problems crop up all the time. For example, five years ago there would have been no demand for smartphone accessories such as the Spiderpodium (one of the case studies we will look at in this chapter) because the problem of not being able to keep your iPhone upright on your car dashboard just didn't exist.

It is very unlikely that you will be the first person ever to have had a specific problem or to have considered a solution to this. Where there is a need, the market will fill it, and as an abundance of free information is available at our fingertips on the internet, gaps in the market can be filled very quickly. The more simple a solution is, the more likely it has already been thought of.

If someone else has already come up with your idea and brought a product to market which is as good as or better than your idea, obviously taking your idea any further is a waste of your time and money.

You can check if your idea is already out there or not using the following methods:

Google

Twenty years ago, market research would have involved trudging around shops or spending hours searching through index cards in a local library. Thanks to internet search engines, it is possible to find out what products are on sale almost everywhere in the world from your sofa (even if the search listings are not in English, Google Translate can translate them for you).

When searching, think of keywords that could be used to describe your idea. This may sound obvious, but most ideas can be described in multiple ways. Finding the best keywords can take time. Try using a thesaurus to help you to come up with alternative words and phrases. Also, don't forget to search for American-English versions of your keywords.

Do a preliminary patent search

Even if you have no intention of applying for a patent for your idea, it is important at this stage to make sure that you will not be infringing anyone else's patent by developing and selling your product.

If someone holds a patent over your idea, or part of it, even if they have never developed it into a product, they could still prevent you from doing so (or could be entitled to a share of your profits).

Using the same keywords as you typed into Google, do a search in the worldwide patent database Espacenet (**worldwide.espacenet.com/advancedSearch**). Usually a quick read of the description of each patent will be enough to find out if the idea behind it is the same as yours.

Searching through patents is time-consuming, but if you are planning on applying for a patent then an initial search of what is already out there is a good way to learn about patents and this will then help you when it comes to applying for your own.

> **Tip**: If you are not confident in searching for patents yourself, there are plenty of organisations who will do it for you for a fee. The British Library offer a paid search service at £87 per hour (plus any online database costs). Email **research@bl.uk** or call 020 7412 7903 if this is something which interests you.
>
> If you employ a professional to search for you, make sure you have a non-disclosure agreement in place before you talk about your invention. You can find a template NDA at:
> **www.productpreneur.co.uk/nda**.

What if no similar products exist?

If you have found that no similar products exist, before popping open the champagne and rushing to file a patent, consider the following questions:

Is it physically possible to make your invention?

It may sound obvious, but there is no point in going any further if your invention won't work. Taking the time to make a first prototype is a good idea in order to make sure your product can be made (see Chapter 3). Also, although your invention may be possible to make, can it be made for a low-enough cost to make your business viable? If each unit costs £100 to make, will people be prepared to pay £200 for the finished product? (See Chapter 4 for an in-depth discussion of pricing.)

Are there any legal restrictions?

Certain kinds of products are tightly regulated – for example, electrical products and toys. If you were to invent a toy for newborn babies with small loose beads, it would not meet European Toy Safety legislation, and you would most likely get into trouble with Trading Standards. Do your research on the legislation which applies to the industry you intend to enter.

Is there a market for your product?

Sometimes there is a good reason why a product doesn't exist – because no one wants to buy it. The timing could be too early – for example, if the iPod had been invented before most households had fast internet access, no one would have bought it as it would have been much easier to buy a CD rather than download MP3s over a slow dial-up connection.

Do thorough market research on whether or not people will be prepared to buy your product before going any further – just be careful not to reveal too much about your product in the process.

What if similar products already exist?

Competition can be a good thing – it is proof that there is already a market for your idea. However, the first product on the market will always have an advantage as it has been around the longest. The longer a product is around, the more consumers become aware of it. Familiarity leads to trust and when it comes to spending money people generally don't like to take risks. Given a choice between two products, one which the consumer has heard of and another which is brand new, most consumers would go for the first option unless there is something really amazing about the second option.

Therefore, if similar products exist, your focus should be on why people would buy your product over more established products. Is it really that different? Is your twist good enough to persuade people to take a risk on a new product?

Detailed market research

Once you have established whether there are any products available that are similar to your idea and made sure that you will not be infringing on anyone else's patent, it is time to do market research and find out from those who matter if your idea really is a good one.

The easiest way to get feedback on your idea is to ask people. However, it has to be the right people. Friends and family may just tell you what you want to hear so it is very important to find people who are impartial.

This can be done as follows:

1. Focus groups/surveys

2. Attend or exhibit at trade shows

3. Ask key buyers directly.

N.B. If your idea is something which can be patented or copyrighted, it is imperative that you put this protection in place before revealing too much about your product to anyone. Keep your mouth firmly shut and head over to Chapter 2.

1. Focus groups/surveys

Focus groups are comprised of individuals who have been carefully selected to provide feedback on your product. Using a focus group is a qualitative form of research, i.e. it is used to assess intangibles like mood and attitude rather than characteristics that can be quantitatively measured.

There are plenty of market research companies around who can find the right people, ask them the right questions and interpret and present the results to you. The advantage of taking this route is that the participants will never have heard of you or your product before and they will give you an unbiased opinion.

The downside is the cost: participants are generally paid for their time and adding this to the market research company's fees it can get quite expensive. This method is more suited to larger companies for this reason.

A cheaper option is to form your own focus group. Gather together a group of people who represent your target buyers, making sure that they are as unbiased as possible (forget asking your mother and best friend). Ask them what they think of your idea. Anonymous questionnaires work well in these situations.

Another good way of doing qualitative research is through a survey. There are many free survey sites available, such as SurveyMonkey (**www.surveymonkey.com**). SurveyMonkey's basic plan is free and it allows you to write a survey with up to ten questions, collect 100 sets of responses and print the results into a PDF document (very useful for including at the end of your business plan). If you are willing to spend £24 per month (at the time of writing), you can make a survey with unlimited responses and will have the ability to download your responses.

Finding people to answer your survey is easy as people love being asked for their opinion. Post links to your survey in internet forums or other websites that your target market will be likely to visit, and post your survey on Facebook or Twitter. A good way to get lots of responses in a short time is to offer a prize to one respondent who you can choose at random – the prize need not to be of a high value, a small e-gift voucher should do the trick.

Writing questions for a survey is surprisingly difficult and requires a lot of trial and error. If your questions are too lengthy or difficult to understand, people won't bother to answer them or will be confused. Be sure to test your questions on your family and friends before letting your survey loose on the world.

2. Attend or exhibit at trade shows

Most industries have several different trade shows each year where buyers go to meet their suppliers and look out for cool new products.

Finding relevant trade shows for your industry is easy: try searching through trade magazines or association websites. Trade shows are not usually open to the public so you may have to register to attend by answering some questions about who you are. Just tell the truth – that you are starting a business in the industry and therefore are a potential future exhibitor at the show.

Once you arrive, don't be shy: talk to anyone and everyone. Keep in mind that the exhibitors are there to sell and have paid a lot of money to be there, so try to arrive at a quiet time (first thing in the morning or last thing in the afternoon) and be prepared to let the exhibitor get away if someone important comes along.

It is difficult to meet retailers when attending a trade show unless you are very lucky and come across them by chance, as they will be walking around like you. Look for friendly people on larger stands: they will be from more established brands with a good knowledge of the industry. They may even be a potential distributor for your product. In any case, any connections you make now will come in handy in the future.

If you already have a prototype of your idea, exhibiting at a trade show is by far the best way to get direct feedback and to meet the big boys of your industry. Patrick Mathews, inventor of the Spiderpodium, took this approach:

> *"It is a capital outlay that you need to invest in. When I looked at how to get into the market, I had read on various forums that it is wise to attend at least two major trade shows in your industry sector, to show that you're serious about your product. We picked up two or three distributors at our very first trade show."*

Exhibiting tips

The following tips will help you make the most of your investment.

Visit the show beforehand if possible

This is a good idea as it will allow you to assess whether it is the right kind of show for your product and to suss out the best areas to take a stand. If this is not possible, talk to people who have exhibited before.

Be choosy when picking a stand

There is nothing worse than being stuck in a quiet corner of the exhibition hall for three days. The best spaces usually go first – look at the popular areas and if you can squeeze in, go for it. Remember that the organisers can usually change the size of a stand, so if you see a good stand but it is too big, ask if it can be split.

Plan your stand well before the show

There are usually two types of stands at an exhibition: shell scheme stands and space-only stands. Most small businesses go for the shell scheme option, which is a ready-made stand with plain white walls. How much you should spend kitting out your stand is a matter of opinion but ask yourself if a few hastily thrown up posters is really going to reflect well on your brand. A better option to cover the shell scheme walls are custom-sized posters which cover the entire panel (choose a background colour other than white if possible). **Printed.com** do custom-sized posters up to 1500x6000mm which is more than large enough to cover the entire shell scheme panels.

If you do go for plain unlaminated posters, you will probably have to throw them away after the show. If you want something you can use more than once, go for rollable PVC graphic panels with a carry case. You can attach them to the shell scheme panels with velcro. Pop-up stands can also look great and are really fast to put up, but they are much more expensive.

Contact buyers before the show

Send a personalised email to all potential buyers during the week before the show inviting them to your stand. Many buyers will have a full schedule of meetings with their existing suppliers and may not have much time to walk around looking for new products. By letting them know about your product beforehand, you are giving yourself an advantage over the hundreds of other exhibitors. The buyers may even make a beeline for your stand if your product really interests them.

Follow up after the show

It may be tempting to give yourself a break after three gruelling days of the show, but it is really important to follow up on every lead, preferably within a few days, so that you are still fresh in people's minds.

Don't be shy

Stop everyone who walks past your stand and tell them about your product. It is surprising how many exhibitors invest thousands of pounds to be at a show and then sit back and watch the world go by. The lady who just walked past may be an exhibition hall cleaner, or she could be the head buyer of John Lewis. Buyers from large stores sometimes hide their badges to avoid getting stopped by everyone.

Enter the awards

Most shows give out awards to exhibitors and it is usually necessary to fill out an application form well before the show. Being shortlisted or winning an award can be a great way to attract attention and draw buyers to your stand, so allocate plenty of time to getting your application right.

Don't get sucked in by negativity

Most trade shows last for three days so it is difficult to keep your momentum up for the whole time, particularly if you are surrounded by jaded fellow exhibitors who complain that the show is 'not as busy as last year' (people say this at *every* show). The best way to stay upbeat is to drink lots of coffee, eat well and bring along an energetic and bubbly friend to help you.

Network with other exhibitors

Although they may enjoy a good moan at times, one of the benefits of exhibiting at a trade show is meeting others in your industry. Introduce yourself to everyone, ask for their advice and share contacts with them.

Remember that other exhibitors may be potential buyers...

...Or business partners. The possibilities for collaboration are endless. Exhibitors will often walk around the show at quiet times so don't be tempted to pack up and leave early.

Most importantly, enjoy the show. As tired as you may feel, be sure to get out and socialise in the evenings. These are the times you will remember afterwards, not the eight solid hours of being on your feet. Just watch how much you drink; there is nothing worse than eight hours on your feet with a stinking hangover!

3. Ask key buyers directly

Although exhibiting at a trade show is undoubtedly the best way to get in front of a large number of buyers in a short time, the second best option is to contact them by phone or email.

The buyers of major retailers are experts in knowing what people want, what will sell and what won't. Buyers typically look after a specific category of products and work up to a year in advance. Their job is to predict what their customers will want before they know themselves.

Major retailers always need new products in order to remain fresh and competitive, so they are interested to hear about good new ideas. Some even invite productpreneurs to pitch: Argos held an open day for toy inventors in 2010 and John Lewis took part in a similar event for all product categories called PitchUp! in 2013. Trade shows sometimes hold award schemes and pitching events where high street buyers are the judges.

If you are not able to attend an open day or pitching event, reaching buyers can be a challenge as retailers do not usually publish their names or contact details on their websites (see Chapter 6 for tips on how to get hold of these). The buyers receive a huge volume of emails and phone calls from new productpreneurs, so getting a response requires persistence.

When contacting buyers, remember that at this stage feedback is what you are looking for rather than a firm order. If the buyer likes your product, the order will come later, but now you simply need their opinion on whether your product will sell, and if and how it can be improved.

Keep your email or call professional and concise – give as much information about your idea as possible, including images, diagrams or whatever you have to hand. Just make sure you have your IP protected before you reveal this detailed information.

How big is the market for your invention?

This is the first question which any potential investor would ask and you need to ask it yourself. Who are your target customers and how many of them are there? It is all very well targeting a niche market, but is the niche big enough to make giving up your day job and starting a new business worthwhile?

In order to find out, you need to ask yourself the following questions.

What problem will your product solve?

This should be an easy question to answer, as for most productpreneurs the problem is something which they have experienced themselves. If your product is a fashion item or a piece of jewellery, the *problem* may be a gap in the market – reasonably-priced haute wedding jewellery or fashion-forward vegetarian shoes, for example.

Claire Mitchell came up with the idea for her product Chillipeeps after being without formula milk while out and about with her young baby. She was able to buy a carton of milk easily from a pharmacy but without a clean, sterilised bottle, there was no way to feed her baby the formula. Chillipeeps is the solution to this problem: it is a pre-sterilised disposable teat which can be attached directly to a carton of formula milk or a bottle of mineral water.

Who are your target customers?

Create a profile of the typical customer who would buy your product. Where do they live? What are their likes and dislikes? How much do they earn?

We could say that Claire Mitchell's target customers are all parents of young babies. However, drilling things down, Chillipeeps is likely to appeal mainly to parents who use formula milk rather than those with babies who are exclusively breastfed. It will also suit sociable parents who like to take their babies out shopping or to visit friends – those who have busy lives and are short of time to prepare formula milk in advance.

Estimate the number of target customers

Usually a quick Google search is enough to estimate just how large your target market is. You could also look at Census data, industry databases and market research reports. Mintel market research reports (**www.mintel.com**) are highly regarded and are available in many public libraries or through Business Link/Gateway (**www.gateway.gov.uk**).

In order to estimate the number of formula-fed babies in the UK, Claire Mitchell could find out UK birth rates by looking at Census data (**www.ons.gov.uk**). She could then estimate the percentage of babies who are given infant formula by looking at breastfeeding statistics from UNICEF.

Come up with a penetration rate

This is the most subjective part of the process. The penetration rate (or market share as it is sometimes known) is the percentage of your target market who will actually buy your product. Even if there are no competitors, the penetration rate will never be 100% as not all of your target market will be aware of the product. Penetration is dependent on the success of your marketing and distribution and is likely to increase over time.

When writing a business plan, the best option is to start with a very low penetration rate and increase it year-on-year as you manage to get your product into more stores and marketing and word-of-mouth kick in to increase sales.

Tip: When calculating your market size, remember that your target market will not be limited to the UK. We live in the EU, where there are no cross-border taxes, so exporting into other countries is very simple. The US is also a huge market, around five times the size of the UK market. International sales will be a route to expansion in later years as your business grows.

Chapter wrap-up

Getting an impartial opinion of whether your product will sell from representatives or experts of your target market, as well as estimating the size of that target market, are crucial steps to help you decide whether to invest further time and money in developing your product.

If people are not convinced about your idea, don't give up right away: listen to the feedback people give you and use it to improve your product. If people hate it or if the target market size is just too small, it is probably time to move on to one of your other ideas (if you are the kind of person who is reading this book, you are bound to have more than one idea).

CHAPTER 2
Protecting Your Idea

BEFORE INVESTING TIME AND money in developing your idea, you need to do everything you can to prevent others from copying it. This is known as protecting your intellectual property – protecting your original ideas and the aspects of your invention that are unique and innovative. Intellectual property protection is not just something which is useful for inventors; design rights/registration, trademarks and copyright can be useful for every kind of productpreneur.

It is equally important to make sure that you will not be infringing upon someone else's intellectual property by selling your product. Even if there are no similar products on the market, if someone holds a patent or design registration over your idea, or even just a part of it, they are entitled to apply for a legal injunction to prevent you from selling your product, or they could even sue you for a share of your profits.

There are four main forms of intellectual property protection that I will discuss in this chapter:

1. A **patent** protects how your product works, how it's made and what it is made of.

2. A **design right/registered design** protects how your product looks.

3. A **trademark** protects your product, business name and slogans.

4. **Copyright** protects your technical sketches, drawings, computer software and sales copy.

It is likely that most or all of the above forms of protection can be used to protect different elements of a product's design or branding.

Let's take a storm-proof umbrella as an example of a product:

- A patent can apply to the way the umbrella is constructed and any unique features, such as an innovative opening mechanism.

- A design right or registration can protect the appearance and shape of the umbrella if it is distinctive enough from the common umbrella shape.

- A trademark can protect the brand and logo of the umbrella and any slogans used to sell it – "Stronger than any storm", etc.

- Copyright can be used for any two-dimensional graphic print on the fabric of the umbrella and the wording of packaging and instructions.

1. Patents

Once you tell people that you have come up with an idea for a new product, the first words you will hear are "Get a patent!" Many people assume that patents are the only way to stop people copying your idea and there is a myth that if you get one, your product will automatically be a big success, making you rich.

Sadly, this is not always the case. Applying for a patent can be incredibly expensive and even if the patent is granted there is no guarantee that your idea will be a success. It has been reported that in the US, 97% of patented inventions make no money.

In order to qualify for a patent, a product must meet the following criteria:

- The invention must be new and not already known to the public.

- The invention must be inventive, i.e. not an obvious modification of what is already known to the public.

- The invention must have an industrial application, i.e. it can be made or used in some kind of industry.

How much does a patent cost?

As patents are specialised legal documents, if you want a strong one that will hold up in court it is necessary to use a patent attorney. As a rough guide, you can expect to pay at least £1500 to have an initial patent application drafted, although patent attorneys charge by the hour, so the more complex your product is, the more you can expect to pay.

After 12 months, to keep the patent application alive, filing national patents or an application under the PCT (patent co-operation treaty) will involve additional costs. Getting to a final stage where patents are granted in several major countries will usually take a number of years and have a total cost of over £10,000. Europe is tricky, as although you can get a main European patent granted, it must also be registered in the individual European countries, which has an extra cost per country. It is hoped that Europe will become a single territory in regard to patents in the future.

In order to save on legal costs, it is a good idea to do as much work as possible yourself and even write a first draft of your patent before consulting a professional. There are lots of very good step-by-step guides which will help you through the process (see the Resources section at the end of this book). Put aside at least a week to learn the ins and outs of patents and the legal terminology in which they are written.

Writing and filing a patent yourself

To save money, some productpreneurs write and file their own patent without ever consulting a professional. This can be a good option if your patent is relatively simple and you are satisfied with UK-only registration, or if you have doubts over whether your invention meets the criteria for a patent and one will ever be granted. Being able to say your invention is *patent-pending* is a good smokescreen that can deter copying.

All that is required for the initial filing of a UK patent is the application form and a full description, along with drawings, of the invention. You file your application online on the Intellectual Property Office's website (**www.ipo.gov.uk**) and you will get a filing receipt which will show the date of filing. This date is very important: it is your priority date. If someone else was to come up with the same idea and file a patent the day after, your patent application will be prior art which will block the subsequent application from being granted.

The first patent application is often called a *priority* patent filing as this establishes the priority date, i.e. the date of the invention. After filing, you will have 12 months to file your claims (the most important part of the patent: the novel and inventive features of your invention).

At the 12-month stage, the priority patent filing must be converted to a full national patent application in as many countries as you can afford, or to a PCT patent application to keep the patent application current. The PCT allows you to file a single international patent application in one language and in accordance with one set of rules, seeking simultaneous patent protection in a number of PCT states. For more information visit the Intellectual Property Office website (**www.ipo.gov.uk/types/patent/p-manage/p-abroad/p-worldwide/p-pct.htm**). If you do not take these steps the application will expire after 12 months and you will have no patent protection.

National or PCT patent applications are usually published after another six months, so your invention will then be there for all to read about on the internet. However, you will still not have full patent protection until the patent application is granted.

Using a professional

Filing a patent by yourself can save money, but if you want a strong patent which will hold up in court in the event of infringement, or if you plan on licensing it to another party, consulting a professional is a must.

Lara Milanova, inventor of Hamster buggy bags, wrote the initial draft of her patent before taking it to a professional:

> *"I found a really good how-to book and wrote my own patent. After I had finished, I contacted a patent attorney and asked if I could hire him for a couple of hours. He said that he hadn't been asked that before but why not. His fee was around £300 per hour. All I wanted him to do was to check that the paper made sense, was logical and covered the areas I wanted it to. I was lucky – after the attorney saw what I had written (and jokingly asked if I wanted a job with him!), he said that looking over it would be an excellent exercise for his trainee. All I gave him in the end was £50! The trainee did all the searches, found some areas that I had missed and made some small changes."*

Finding a patent attorney

As with finding any advisor or supplier, personal recommendation is the best way. Join an invention forum and network with other inventors. Ask them which patent attorney they used and if they would recommend them. Keep in mind that it is important to find a patent attorney who specialises in the right area.

The Chartered Institute of Patent Attorneys holds regular clinics given by its members at libraries across the UK to provide free basic advice to inventors. See their website for details of where the clinics are held (**www.cipa.org.uk/pages/advice-clinics**). If you are not based in any of these cities, many patent attorneys offer a free 40-minute initial session, so contact one in your area to ask about this.

Tip: "The good thing about a patent attorney is that they can broaden your original idea. Your idea may be for one application but actually it could have a number of applications." Claire, Chillipeeps

---

What if you can't get a patent?

A patent is not the only way to protect a product from being copied. Even patented products will be copied if they are successful enough. Sometimes an infringer will design a product around a patent, while other times they will take a gamble on the patent holder not being able to afford to sue.

A big plus is that if your product is not patentable, there are no restrictions on telling people about it (although use your common sense – don't reveal everything and be careful who you talk to). This will make your market research a lot easier: you can even produce a small run of your product and ask people to test it before investing in a large quantity of stock. Another bonus is that you will probably be able to get your product on to the market faster and keep a step ahead of your competitors.

There are three other ways to protect your intellectual property which you can consider.

2. Design rights/registration

As opposed to a patent, which protects the function of an invention, a design right or registration protects its appearance.

Design rights are automatic – as soon as a three-dimensional design is created, it is automatically protected by an unregistered design right for up to 15 years in the UK. However, as there is no formal registration of the design, proving the date of creation would be difficult in the event of a dispute. Also, if someone else were to come up with the same design, it would be necessary to prove that they copied the unregistered design in order to prove that an infringement had occurred.

A better option to protect a design is to formally register it. Design registration can protect two-dimensional designs or surface patterns, as well as the three-dimensional shape.

To be valid for design registration, a design must:

- Be new – no earlier identical design can have been made available to the public.

- Have individual character – the overall impression it produces on the *informed user* must be different from the overall impression produced on such a user by any design which has previously been made available to the public.

The *informed user* is someone who will be aware of the designs in the industry concerned and will possess a certain degree of knowledge regarding the usual features of those designs. Using mobile phones as an example, an informed user would be someone who takes a particular interest in mobiles and can differentiate between brands and styles, but they would not be a mobile phone designer.

The process of getting a design registration is surprisingly quick when compared to getting a patent: the registration is usually examined and granted within a few months of the initial application. This is because design applications in the UK and EU are not examined.

Unlike the situation with patents, you do not have to keep your design secret in order to be eligible for design registration. There is a grace period in the UK and EU of up to 12 months to test or try out the design before registering it.

Although designs can be registered with the Intellectual Property Office (IPO), it is also possible to register your design in the whole of the EU with the Office for Harmonization in the Internal Market (OHIM). This option may make more sense if you plan on selling your idea abroad. The cost of applying for one design through the OHIM is €350, plus any professional fees.

How effective is a design registration?

In the UK, it has been estimated that only 15% of designs are formally registered, which suggests that businesses do not have much confidence in design registration.

However, design registration is used extensively and successfully in the fashion industry. Jimmy Choo is a company well known for aggressively protecting its intellectual property. The company has taken action against New Look for copying its Bonbon shoe and Marks & Spencer for selling a £9.50 imitation of its £495 Cosmo evening bag. Both matters settled out of court for an undisclosed amount and both high street retailers withdrew and destroyed all of the offending stock as a result.

Even though small businesses may not have the funds of Jimmy Choo to take a large retailer to court, registering a design can act as a deterrent to potential infringers. A registration indicates the owner has made an investment in registering the design and therefore is likely to take infringement more seriously. Writing to an alleged infringer and putting them on notice of design registrations may be sufficient to stop the infringement.

Keira O'Mara, inventor of Mamascarf, a breastfeeding cover, has successfully put off several imitators by sending them a cease-and-desist letter (a standard letter written by a lawyer advising the infringer of the existence of the design registration). Keira admits that had the infringers been larger companies with access to their own lawyers, they may not have been put off so easily.

3. Trademarks

A trademark is a sign which can distinguish your goods and services from those of your competitors (you may refer to your trademark as your *brand*). It can be words, a logo or a combination of both.

No matter what industry your business operates in, registering your business name and product name as trademarks is crucial as it will prevent others using those names and it will help to distinguish your products.

Before choosing a name for your business and product, it is important to do a trademark search to ensure that no one else has registered that name before. Online searches can be carried out on the UK IPO website (for UK trademarks) and the OHIM website (for Community trademarks in the European Union).

When coming up with a name for your product and business, it is important to note that a name cannot be trademarked if it:

- Simply describes your invention.

- Has become customary in your particular industry.

- Is not distinctive.

- Is offensive.

- Is against the law.

- Is deceptive.

For example, I hold a trademark for the term 'Safebreathe' in the context of toys. I would not have been able to trademark the term 'Breathable' for the toys as it is too descriptive. I also would not have been able to register the term 'Soft' as it is customary in the toy industry to refer to stuffed toys as 'soft toys'.

When applying for a trademark, you will need to provide a list of the goods and/or services on which you intend to use your trademark. You then need to decide under which classes to apply. These *classes* are categories covering different types of products, so for example in the UK "articles made of wood" would come under Class 20. A list of classes can be found at **oami.europa.eu/ec2**. Your trademark will be restricted to those classes under which you apply.

My 'Safebreathe' trademark is for Class 28, which covers toys, meaning that I have a monopoly over the term when used for toys. However, other trademark holders have a monopoly over 'Safebreathe' for other types of products, such as paint and medicine.

A UK trademark costs £170 to file online (or £200 if you use the Right Start service from the IPO, **www.ipo.gov.uk/types/tm/t-applying/t-before/t-cost/rightstart.htm**). The trademark office will issue an examination report setting out any objections to application and will provide a deadline for responding to any such objections. With Right Start, you pay £100 at the time of filing, the trademark is examined and you will receive an examination report. You then have the chance to decide whether to go ahead with the application. If it turns out that the trademark is unlikely to be granted, you can choose not to go ahead, saving yourself the extra £70 which you would have paid had you not used the Right Start option.

Once the application is accepted, it is advertised in the official *Trade Marks Journal*. For UK and Community trademark applications, the trademark registry reviews the trademark register to check for potential conflicts with existing marks. If any are found, the prior trademark owner will be notified and has the right to oppose any application once it has been advertised.

After the application has been advertised, third parties have a period of two to three months to oppose the application if they believe it conflicts with an earlier trademark or right. If no oppositions are filed or any oppositions are successfully overcome, the mark will be registered and a certificate of registration will be issued.

If you are planning to operate your business outside the UK, the best option is to file a Community trademark through the Office of Harmonization in the Internal Market (OHIM).

This can be done through the OHIM website (**oami.europa.eu/ows/rw/pages/QPLUS/forms/electronic/fileApp licationCTM.en.do**). The cost of filing a single Community trademark online is €900. The Community trademark can be used as a basis for an international trademark through the World Intellectual Property Organization (WIPO).

The importance of applying for a trademark is demonstrated by a saga involving the well-known wartime phrase 'Keep Calm and

Carry On'. In 2000, the phrase was rediscovered by a small bookstore in Northumberland called Barter Books who found an old wartime 'Keep Calm' poster in their attic.

Barter Books began to sell the posters but never registered the phrase as a trademark, believing that it was an old saying which was in general use. The phrase has since appeared on everything from biscuit tins to t-shirts and notepads.

In 2012, an opportunistic supplier of Keep Calm merchandise, Keep Calm and Carry On Ltd., was controversially granted a Community trademark for the phrase despite having being refused a UK trademark. Although the Community trademark is now the subject of a legal dispute, Keep Calm and Carry On Ltd. has succeeded in creating a monopoly for itself, as eBay has now banned all Keep Calm merchandise other than merchandise supplied by Keep Calm and Carry On Ltd. from its site.

4. Copyright

Copyright is an automatic right which arises whenever an individual or company creates a work. In the context of product creation, copyright can protect the expression of your idea – the technical sketches, drawings, computer software and sales copy (the wording on your website, brochures and packaging).

The only criteria for qualifying for copyright protection is that the work should be regarded as original and should exhibit a degree of labour, skill or judgement.

The © 'C in a circle' is the normal copyright symbol, but whether the symbol is used or not will not change the fact that copyright exists in the work. It is, however, strongly recommended that you include the symbol on your work if at all possible so as to deter copyright infringement.

Copyright law has been used somewhat successfully by Julie Deane, founder of the Cambridge Satchel Company, a range of bright and funky versions of the classic satchel. Julie alleged that the former factory which produced her satchels used her patterns to start their own satchel brand, Zatchels, and in 2011 she filed a suit for copyright infringement. Although the case didn't reach court, the Cambridge Satchel Company received an undisclosed sum of damages from its former manufacturer.

***

In addition to the four formal methods of protecting intellectual property, there are also a couple of informal ways to discourage imitators:

Confidentiality agreements

Trade secrets – such as manufacturing processes or recipes for food – can be difficult to protect formally, but keeping them a secret can be the strongest form of protection from copying. Confidentiality agreements, unlike patents, can last forever. Assuming that the trade secret was not already common knowledge, if your confidentiality agreement is breached you have a right to sue.

First-mover advantage

Some believe that the best tactic to discourage copying is to get a product on to the market before anyone else. The long process of getting a patent can delay a product launch and, for high-tech products, by the time a patent is granted the product may already be obsolete.

If your product is the first of its kind, it will always be the original. You will be a step ahead of your competitors at putting your product in front of your target customers' noses through marketing and distribution. When given the choice of two similar products, consumers are likely to go for the one which is well-known and trusted unless there is something very special about the newer product.

As a former jewellery designer, with her wedding jewellery in stores such as Liberty, Claire Yarwood-White operated in an industry where it is notoriously difficult to formally protect work:

> "Yes, I did have incidents of people copying my work. Sometimes you could tell a design had been 'inspired by' one of mine but I tended to give the benefit of the doubt in those situations. Even if there was a clear copy of a design, I would usually let it go, on the basis that it might be a much smaller or less established business that didn't pose any real threat. Also, because of the type of jewellery I produced, which was quite commercial, I did take the position that in some cases you couldn't really own the design. For example, a simple pair of pearl earrings, or a crystal pendant, would be a 'classic' design and very hard to claim copyright on."

Claire was more concerned with stopping others from copying her branding materials:

> "Because of the difficulty in protecting my designs, I put a great value on my branding and marketing materials as unique. On a couple of occasions I did have to write polite letters to people to let them know that I was aware that my marketing materials were being copied. This seemed to be all that was required to stop the practice. I think in most cases copying takes place when people lack inspiration or the vision for their own businesses, so I tend not to see those people as a threat, and instead concentrate my energies on staying one step ahead of the rest of the market."

Chapter wrap-up

The strongest way to formally protect your product is through a patent. If your product meets the criteria, applying for a patent is risky due to the expense and the fact that there is no guarantee that you will ever be able to recoup your investment. However, if you are looking to licence your idea, a strong patent is a must.

If your product is not eligible for a patent, there are three other ways you can protect the intellectual property involved with it – through design registration, trademarks and copyright. Some informal methods to consider are confidentiality agreements and getting your product on to the market fast in order to have the advantage of being the first to do so.

CHAPTER 3
Manufacturing and Prototypes

AFTER COMING UP WITH your idea, naturally one of the first things to think about is what your product will be made from and who will make it.

Some products, particularly those that are sewn or made from fabric, may never need any professional design help. Maybe you have already started off making and selling your designs by yourself. My first product, the Cot Wrap, fell into this category. I sourced the fabric from a supplier in China and had a local seamstress sew up a prototype, which I then took along to a trade show.

While this is fine for selling small-scale directly to customers through Etsy or at craft fairs, if you are going to supply a major retailer you will have to outsource manufacturing at some point, in order to make enough units of your product and to free up your time to concentrate on running your business.

For more technically complex products, you will probably need the help of a professional designer. Before getting any outside help, be sure to protect your intellectual property (see Chapter 2). Once you have filed a patent, you are free to talk about your invention with anyone and everyone.

Producing your product for a low enough price to make you and your retailers a profit, whilst maintaining a high enough quality to satisfy picky high street buyers, is a huge challenge. For many labour-intensive products, manufacturing in the UK is not viable unless your product is considered a luxury item and customers are willing to pay a high price for it.

A prototype is basically an example or a mock-up of the finished product. If your product is not something which can be produced economically on a small scale, a prototype is essential for showing prospective retailers how your product will look and work and to help you decide whether or not to invest in expensive tooling. Making a prototype can be as simple as getting out your sewing machine and using old clothes to create a mock-up of your product. Alternatively, you may have to employ a professional manufacturer, as discussed above.

No one will expect a prototype to be identical to the finished product. It need not even be made of the same materials as the finished product will be. Even if your product is very complex, it is usually a good idea to make some kind of mock-up yourself before consulting a professional, in order to help explain your vision. You may need to be a bit inventive in order to do this – look at the materials you can find in your home and at your local DIY store.

> **Tip**: If your invention is made of plastic it is possible to make a mock-up using a product called Shapelock (**www.shapelock.com**). This is a kind of plastic which melts in hot water, allowing you to mould it, and then goes rigid when at room temperature.

Sometimes it is necessary to make a prototype before filing a patent in order to test out an idea – to make sure it works and that it can be produced for a low enough cost – before spending money on a patent attorney. If this is the case for your invention, make sure that you ask your prototype maker to sign a non-disclosure agreement (NDA). A sample NDA can be downloaded from **www.productpreneur.co.uk/nda**.

Design
Finding a professional designer

Personal recommendation is always the best way to find any supplier or professional help. Network with others in your industry and find out who they used. Look for products similar to yours and find out who designed them – if the product creator is happy with their designer, they should be willing to share their details with you.

Be sure to look for a designer who has experience in your particular area (or who is willing to learn in their own time – sometimes enthusiasm can make up for lack of experience). If you have a patent, it is very important that the designer fully understands it.

If you aren't able to find a designer on personal recommendation, ask for references and follow them up. It is best to find a designer who has worked with inventors before rather than only large companies – this means that they will understand the unique challenges that lone inventors face (which are mainly financial).

Lastly, make sure you choose someone who you can get on well with and who responds to your requests promptly and professionally – you will be spending a lot of time with them and spending a lot of money on this person, so you want the experience to be as stress-free as possible.

Claire Mitchell, inventor of Chillipeeps, recommends that productpreneurs use a local design company:

> *"You need to have somebody that's down the road that you can pop in to see, have proper meetings with and understand what they are doing."*

Marc Ward, creator of the Jamm door wedge, used a local university:

> *"I rang around a few injection moulding companies and they pointed me to a facility at a local university where they do prototyping. You can go to Falmouth University with your idea and they have all the knowledge and tools to turn it into reality. It's a fantastic place. It's not free, you have to pay for it, but you can walk out of there with a rapid prototype and CAD drawings and then you can take them wherever you want. You're then speaking the language of the professionals. We used our prototype to have an aluminium mould made."*

A warning

While the majority of product designers and prototype-making companies are honest, the industry also attracts fraudsters and scammers. This is made worse by the fact that in the UK there is no oversight body to monitor such companies.

Be very wary of using one company to help you to research your idea, obtain a patent and to bring your invention to market. These are very different specialist areas and it is best to keep them separate. If you are using the same company for everything, they have a big incentive to tell you that your idea is fantastic in order to encourage you to carry on with the process, so that they continue to make money from you.

The product design process

The first stage of the product design process is writing a brief for your designer. Be sure to go into as much detail as possible – a quick paragraph will not be sufficient. Remember that the designer will be charging you for their time: if you give them free rein they are likely to go off on a tangent, wasting time and money for both of you.

Having said this, it is best to expect some drift from the brief – as the designer is likely to have more experience of developing products than you, they will come up with ideas and issues that you will not have considered.

The brief should include the following:

- **Background** – the potential customer, the competitors and the industry that the product will be part of.

- **Project objectives** – what you want to achieve and how the design will be used.

- **Constraints on the design** – safety standards, packaging requirements.

- **Target cost** – you should have a per-unit production cost in mind that takes into account your target retail price and the margin which you and your suppliers require (see Chapter 6).

- **Project management** – budgets, schedule and deadlines.

- **Intellectual property** – establishing who owns IP rights to the designs being produced.

The next stage is idea generation – the designer should come up with a number of concepts and present these to you. You can then talk through these together and decide which concept to develop. It is a good idea to specify exactly how many concepts the designer will present to you at the outset.

The concepts will usually be presented as a CAD (computer-aided design) and then one or more will be developed into a full 3D prototype. This prototype will then be tested extensively and you will have the chance to show it to potential retailers and customers.

Rapid prototyping

In the past, making a prototype often involved expensive injection moulding and could take months. Nowadays it is possible to get a prototype in a day thanks to rapid prototyping – a printing process that uses layers to create a three-dimensional mock-up.

Rapid prototyping involves using a 3-D computer-aided design program to create the object for printing. Once the file has been transferred to the printer, printer software digitally slices the object into very thin cross-sections called layers. During the print process, the 3-D printer starts at the bottom of the design and builds up successive layers of material until the object is finished.

Different 3-D printers use different materials to build layers. Some use liquid polymer or gel, others use resin (which tends to be more expensive).

Patrick Mathews of Breffo used rapid prototyping to create his first model of the Spiderpodium:

> *"The product itself requires very specific types of steel, wire and rubber so that it doesn't snap. Before making an investment in tooling, I had a design team create the visual look and technical specifications of the product and sent these through to a rapid prototyping team who were able to churn out a prototype within a few days. It was a non-working prototype but looked very similar to what I wanted. We went to a trade show with the prototype and the level of interest convinced me to take the product to the next level, which of course required investment in tooling."*

Drawings

Formal drawings of your product can be useful at several stages in the process of product creation. Patent drawings are required along with a patent application to explain how the invention works. CAD (computer-aided design) drawings are necessary to make 3-D virtual prototypes which, as I have just discussed, are useful to show to potential buyers.

Technical drawings are essential to obtain production quotes from manufacturers. Potential manufacturers will need to understand exactly how to make the product and in what dimensions. A good technical drawing completed by a trained engineer will be drawn in accordance with universal standards for everything from layout, line thickness, symbols, descriptive geometry, text size, notation, dimensioning and view projections. This means that anyone similarly qualified can look at the drawing and understand exactly how to make your product.

In the past, technical drawings were created with pencil, paper, protractors and triangles. These days they are done on computers using CAD software such as AutoCAD or SolidWorks.

Tooling

If your product is made from plastic, metal, glass or rubber, you will probably need an injection mould for mass production. An injection mould is a block of metal (aluminium or steel) with a cavity that is created in the shape of your product.

The material which your product is made from is heated and fed into the cavity where it cools and hardens into the right shape. When hard, it is ejected from the mould and, voilà, a unit of your product has been produced.

This process is repeated, mainly automatically by machines, for the whole order. If your product consists of a number of separate parts, a separate mould is usually needed for each part. This explains why tooling can be the most expensive part of creating a product.

Manufacturing

Finding a good and reliable manufacturer is essential for the success of your product. No matter how successful you are at marketing and selling it, if you don't have enough actual units of your product at the right quality to meet demand, you have wasted your time and money.

Finding the perfect manufacturing partner for your business can take time. Most manufacturers prefer to work with large, established companies who order in large volumes, rather than new productpreneurs with small volumes, so you are going to have to convince them that you can generate large orders in the future.

On the other side of the coin, you need to find a manufacturer who can produce your product for a low enough price without sacrificing quality and a quick production time. It needs to be a win-win situation for both parties: if you knock the price down too low, the manufacturer has a big incentive to cut corners with quality and give priority to more profitable orders.

What kind of factory to look for

The most difficult part of the process of finding a manufacturer can sometimes be identifying exactly what kind of factory you need to look for. For example, if your product is sewn, should you look for a textile manufacturer or a sewing contractor? It really depends – the Cot Wrap is made in China by a textile manufacturer that outsources the sewing to a small local factory. However, in the UK, a textile manufacturer would be very unlikely to do this.

Tip: Choosing a manufacturer as close to home as possible will save a lot of headaches. If you are lucky enough to find one in your city, you will hopefully have short lead times (the lag between placing an order and receiving the finished product), without having to wait for your product to be transported. You will also be able to pop in and take a look at the process and check that everything is being done the way you want it to be.

Labour-intensive products

Textile products are an example of items which are largely made by hand rather than machines, so they could be described as more labour-intensive.

The good news with labour-intensive products is that the start-up costs can be quite low, as no investment in tooling is required. If your product is made from materials which are easily obtainable, you will be able to test the market by making a small quantity.

The bad news is that in the UK, labour costs are relatively high. As a result, almost all sewn products are made overseas, usually in China, India or Eastern Europe. The exception, of course, being luxury and designer products which consumers are willing to pay a premium for.

For example, if making a simple teddy in the UK costs £10, you will have to sell it for £30 to £40 to make a large enough margin (see Chapter 4). The same teddy could be made in China for £3 and then you would then be able to sell it for £9 to £12.

Products made in China have a bad reputation, but not many people would realistically pay £40 for a teddy. When I was looking into toy manufacturers for Safebreathe toys, I didn't find any soft toys which are made on a large scale in the UK (with the exception of collector's teddies, which are not really toys for children). There is a niche market for UK-made toys on websites like Etsy, but part of the charm is that they are handmade especially for each order – there is usually a wait time while the toy is physically made.

Manufacturing overseas is cheaper, but factories normally have a very high minimum order quantity. Starting up a production line for a new product is costly: large orders are much more economical for the factory and they will also get quantity discounts for the raw materials.

For example, the minimum order for soft toys is generally 5000 units. However, you may be able to convince a factory to do a smaller run if they believe that it is a test run and larger orders will follow in the future.

Machine-intensive products

Although machine-intensive products typically require tooling, which can be a huge investment, the good news is that because machines do most of the work rather than people, manufacturing in the UK can be viable. Even if China works out a little cheaper, the three-month lead times and difficulty in monitoring quality can make manufacturing at home a better option.

It is common for manufacturers to help productpreneurs find a company to make the tooling. If you, the product creator, are paying for the tooling (which should be the case unless you are happy for your manufacturer to use the tooling to make products for your competitors), it is crucial that you have a tooling agreement in place.

You, the product creator, need to have title to both the design of the tooling and the tooling itself. This means that you will have the flexibility to change suppliers (and take the tooling with you) and you will be protected if the manufacturer goes bankrupt. As the stakes are so high, it is best to get an agreement drafted by a lawyer.

How to find a manufacturer

Here are four ways to find a manufacturer:

Networking

As I've said throughout, personal recommendation is always the best way to find business associates. Join networking groups and online forums, and become active on Twitter. Seek out those who produce similar products (although not direct competitors) and ask if they would recommend their manufacturer.

Be warned: some may be reluctant to share their factory's details. Finding a good manufacturer is like finding a great restaurant hidden away in a city full of the mediocre. Should you tell the world so they can all turn up and make it so busy that you can never get a table? Or should you keep it to yourself? Also, from their perspective, it can be a risk to refer people who they don't know, because if the person referred turns out to be a time-waster it can reflect badly on them.

Sourcing agents

Agents can be useful if your product is complicated or if you feel completely overwhelmed at the prospect of dealing with manufacturers yourself. Using an agent can also speed up the process considerably, if you just don't have the time. Agents will charge either a fixed fee or a small percentage of each order and will usually take care of arranging everything from manufacturing to shipping and even warehousing.

Again, personal recommendation is the best way to find a good agent. If this is not possible, sourcing agents can be found easily online. Meet a number of agents personally and ask them for references before choosing one to work with.

B2B websites

There are numerous websites which provide a platform to find manufacturers. Alibaba (**www.alibaba.com**) is probably the most well known, but it is also the most notorious for being used by scammers.

Other similar websites are Global Sources (**www.globalsources.com**), HKTDC (**www.hktdc.com**) and Tradekey (**www.tradekey.com**), all of which are supposedly more reputable than Alibaba. All of these sites are mainly focused on Chinese manufacturers, although there are UK manufacturers too if you look hard enough.

The main problem with using these kinds of websites is that it is hard to be sure just who you are dealing with. It would be very easy for anyone to set themselves up as a manufacturer on these websites when really they are an agent who buys goods from numerous factories and sells them to foreigners at huge mark ups.

Even worse, a scammer who has absolutely nothing at all to sell could set themselves up as a manufacturer and disappear after taking your money. Just do an internet search for 'Alibaba' and 'scammers' and you will see that this happens a lot, although mainly with high-value electrical items such as iPhones.

Of course there are a lot of honest manufacturers on these sites too. It is just important to check them out properly before handing over any money.

Google

Use Google to search for a manufacturer as a last resort. The problem is that the result that shows up at the top of the search rankings may not be the best manufacturer, just the most computer literate. Many good manufacturers do not have a state-of-the-art web presence so you will not find them in an internet search.

Also, when I was looking for a manufacturer, I found it quite difficult to figure out what search terms to use. For my textile product, 'contract sewing' and 'cut make trim' came up with good results, but I wouldn't automatically have thought of these terms at first.

***

Finding a good manufacturer takes time, unless you are extremely lucky and strike gold with the first call you make. You will hear many horror stories (I could tell you a few myself), so it pays to be cautious and take your time.

The whole process of getting a quote can be slow, as most manufacturers will require both a finished sample and the raw materials so they can work out how much they can make the product for. From their point of view costing takes time so a lot of patience and gentle reminders may be required.

Quality

Almost every product creator will have stories to tell about receiving defective units and having to spend days, weeks and months sorting through batches and fixing products. There are ways to minimise the risk of getting a problem batch:

- **Product specifications** – You need to explicitly spell out the level of quality (down to the little details) that you expect from the manufacturer. It is best to do this in writing. Writing product specifications is difficult, as you need to be able to foresee everything which could go wrong or that could be misinterpreted. The product specifications for the Cot Wrap cover the exact size of each stitch, the requirement to ensure that there are no loose threads left uncut and even the text size on the care label.

- **Final samples** – You are likely to receive many samples from your manufacturer before you are completely happy with the product. Be sure to inspect each sample thoroughly, test it and pull it apart to make sure it can't be broken easily. Once you have resolved all issues, ask for three final samples. Label the samples, take photos of them and send one back to the manufacturer, making it clear that you have signed it off as the agreed standard upon which mass production will be based. Keep one of the samples for yourself and send the other to the company who will be doing your quality control (if applicable).

- **Quality control** – When using a manufacturer for the first time, it is best to visit (or send in an impartial quality control company to visit) as many times as possible. This means that any problems can be identified right away rather than after production has been completed. Production units can be chosen at random and compared to the final, signed-off sample. It is common for a final inspection to be carried out before an order is paid for and dispatched.

- **Relationship** – If the manufacturer thinks that you are a serious customer who will bring lots of future work to them, they are likely to take your order more seriously than a one-off order from a novice. Present yourself professionally and try to appear bigger than you are – see Chapter 5 for more tips on this.

Chapter wrap-up

Finding a good manufacturer to make your product on a large scale is scary. You may have to pay upfront for a large order and there is always an element of risk that something will go wrong. Most manufacturers are eager to do a good job and gain future business, but if you fail to specify exactly what you expect then you could find that their idea of a good job varies significantly from yours.

Manufacturers have the difficult task of motivating their workers, who are often low paid and carry out menial, uninteresting tasks, and are constantly under pressure to keep costs down by working fast. This is when quality can slip. The best tactic is to choose your manufacturer wisely, communicate clearly exactly what you want and invest time and money in quality control to minimise the chance of something bad happening.

CHAPTER 4
Funding and Running Your Business

IN THIS CHAPTER I will go over the basics which you need to consider when starting a business, including how to get funding, pricing your product, company structure, cash flow and finance, and keeping on the right side of product safety law.

With any business, bringing a product to market requires investment in the beginning to start things off. Thanks to the global economic downturn which began in 2008, the traditional way of financing a business – a bank loan – has been increasingly difficult to access. As a result, new forms of finance have sprung up, such as crowdfunding.

Although most productpreneurs start their own businesses to manufacture and sell their products, some are lucky enough to license their product to someone else. Licensing is every inventor's dream: letting someone else do all the hard work while sitting back and watching the royalties pour in.

Unfortunately, very few productpreneurs succeed in licensing their invention and even if they do the royalties are usually very low, as the licensee needs to be compensated for taking on all the risk and responsibility. Starting your own business around your invention allows you to receive a larger chunk of the rewards.

Funding

Launching a product is expensive, especially if you apply for a patent, use a product designer and have to invest in tooling. I have noticed that in the nursery products industry, the vast majority of productpreneurs are former city high-fliers with big savings accounts and people who have already run a successful business before. Of course, there are exceptions; I have met some very inspiring people who have achieved a great deal through resourcefulness and sheer hard work.

Not every kind of product is prohibitively expensive to create: textile products are easy to launch without investing lots of money. However, it is still necessary to invest money in design, branding and marketing in order to present your product in the right way and let the world know that it exists.

Bank finance

It used to be the case that the first thing a product creator would do when looking for funding was book an appointment with their bank manager. However, things have changed since 2008 when the global economic downturn began. Banks have become increasingly risk-averse and getting a loan without some form of security has become near impossible.

The reluctance of banks to finance new businesses has been addressed by the government through its Enterprise Finance Guarantee scheme (previously known as the Small Loans Guarantee Scheme), where the government underwrites 75% of the loan. In practice, the scheme should make it easier for small businesses without collateral to get loans. Unfortunately, the scheme has not been a big success. Many banks find that it has too much paperwork and they aren't prepared to risk the remaining 25% of the loan on small businesses.

If you do decide to approach banks for loans, you will need a very robust business plan, including cash and profit forecasts, to satisfy the bank that it will get its money back.

The bank will want to know exactly what you intend to spend the loan on, so calculate how much you will ask for very carefully. Chances are you will also have to present a personal guarantee to repay the loan – prepare a list of all of your assets, including property, savings, cars and your salary minus your expenses. Be prepared to go to as many banks as possible.

It is usually much easier to get an overdraft than a bank loan. With an overdraft, you will have the advantage of being able to only draw what you need, and only paying interest on this. However, the interest rate will be much higher than on a loan, and overdrafts can be called in at any time, making them a risky form of finance. Overdrafts are better suited for day-to-day running expenses rather than for start-up costs.

Some productpreneurs even use credit cards to pay for their start-up costs, making the most of interest-free offers by transferring the balance frequently.

Government grants/loans

Government grants and loans are usually given to companies who will create jobs, exports, innovations or environmental benefits. The common perception of grants is that they are *free money*. However, in reality this is not the case. I was lucky enough to receive a marketing grant from my local council when I started Safe Dreams. Getting the grant involved months of work creating a strong business plan which would convince the council that with their grant I could grow the business large enough to create local jobs.

Grants are typically matched funding, covering 30% to 50% of expenses. This means that for every £1 which you receive, you will need to have already spent £1 of your own money (and have produced evidence of this). There can be a significant time lag between spending money and being reimbursed through the grant, which can make managing cash flow difficult.

Incubators

Business incubators are programmes designed to support the development of innovative companies through investment, business support resources and services. An example is Seed Camp (**www.seedcamp.com**), which invests in 20 companies each year, providing them with office space, mentoring and a €50,000 investment in return for a 10% stake.

Venture capitalists/business angels

Venture capitalists (VCs) invest in high-risk, high-return start ups. Similar to VCs, business angels are wealthy entrepreneurs looking to invest in new businesses. This type of funding is not easy to get but it may be relevant if your invention is something revolutionary which is likely to generate a huge profit. The investment made is usually over £1m, in return for a share of equity (and sometimes also debt).

Crowdfunding

Crowdfunding is an innovative new trend in business funding which has sprung up in the wake of the popularity of social media. It involves pitching for funds from the general public (the crowd).

Kickstarter (**www.kickstarter.com**), the first crowdfunding site, is focused on creative projects, mainly in film, games, music, art, design and technology. Crowdfunder (**www.crowdfunder.com**) is a newer, UK-based site where all kinds of businesses can pitch for between £1k and £50k.

Both sites have "All or nothing" rules for funding: if a project's stated funding goal isn't met in the time given to raise the money then none of the prospective funders are charged and the project doesn't receive any funds. This makes pitchers think twice about asking for too much funding and protects (to a certain extent) the funders from throwing money at projects that will never come to fruition.

In order to be successful in crowdfunding, you will need to create a professional video pitch and work hard sharing it through social media.

Other ideas for raising funds

- If you are under 30, the **Prince's Trust** (**www.princes-trust.org.uk**) provides loans of up to £4000 to help those who are unemployed to start a business.

- **Personal finance** – The easiest way to raise money is by using your assets – your home, car, etc. – as collateral for a loan (or a mortgage). This is risky but the threat of losing your home is definitely an incentive to work hard.

- **Family/friends** – If you want to stay friends, be sure to have a written loan agreement to avoid any misunderstandings.

- **Dragons' Den** – The Dragons are essentially business angels (see above). Getting on to the programme means going though many rounds of interviews and hanging around a TV studio for days while running the risk of your pitch ending up on the editing room floor. The upside is that even if you don't succeed in getting investment, having your product appear on TV can be the best form of publicity (assuming that the Dragons don't tear it apart).

The complex issue of pricing

Many productpreneurs fail to give enough thought to setting a price for their product. If you were to only ever sell your product directly to consumers, setting a price would be easy. It would simply be a case of balancing how much profit you want to make with how much consumers are willing to pay.

However, selling large volumes of your product will only be possible if you bring in other parties to help you to sell: distributors, wholesalers, retailers and/or sales agents. Each party you bring in needs to make enough profit or they won't bother to waste shelf or warehouse space on your product. Therefore, you need to set your suggested retail price high enough to allow each party in the chain to make enough profit. You need to find out how much margin each party expects and make sure that you can afford to give it to them.

The end goal of every business is to make a profit. In order to assess whether your business will be profitable, you need to know how much it will cost you to make your product and assess how much a consumer would pay for it. If the difference is large enough to leave enough profit for yourself and all the other parties in your chain, your business is viable. If not, move on and look for new opportunities.

I look at some elements of pricing below.

Cost price

The cost price is the actual cost of producing a single unit of your product. It will include the price which your manufacturer charges you plus any shipping costs, import tariffs and any other costs involved in physically getting your product to your warehouse.

> **Tip**: As the size of your orders increases, your cost price is likely to become lower due to economies of scale. Therefore, it is useful to ask your manufacturer what the production price would be for larger orders.

(Recommended) retail price

When selling your product direct to consumers, you are able to choose exactly what price you wish to sell it at (the *retail* price). However, if you are selling through stockists you are only allowed to *recommend* a price. You, as the manufacturer, are not allowed to dictate a price at which your products can be sold by stockists due to anti-price fixing legislation. If you were to do so, you could be reported to the Office of Fair Trading (OFT), which has the power to fine companies.

Your stockists are therefore free to sell your product at whatever price they want. This can be incredibly frustrating for you as a product creator. If one stockist sells your product at a price lower than its RRP, all of your other stockists have to choose between losing sales, lowering the price themselves and sacrificing profit, or dropping your product altogether.

Bear in mind that it is much easier to lower your price than to raise it. Unexpected costs always crop up in business so it is wise to give yourself as big a cushion as possible. There are lots of ways to lower your price, as people love a bargain – promotional prices, special offers, multi-buy discounts, etc.

Finding out the highest price that the market will bear can be done through the methods we discussed in Chapter 2 – surveys, focus groups, and by asking buyers and potential customers directly.

Look at the prices which your competitors are charging, although don't be tempted to get into a price war with them. Remember that your product is different from anything else on the market (or you wouldn't be wasting your time), and consumers will pay a premium for this difference. It can be scary charging a higher price than anyone else, but sometimes you need to in order to signal to consumers that your product is better.

I learned this lesson the hard way. I set the RRP of the Cot Wrap at the same level as one of its competitors, but the price was discounted online and it ended up being a few pounds cheaper. The Cot Wrap is better in quality – it is thicker (which means more protection against bumps) and has a 100% cotton inner surface rather than polyester.

I remember reading a review on Amazon from a customer who was disappointed with the quality of the Cot Wrap (you can't please everyone) and wrote that she wished she had spent a few pounds extra and bought the competing product. The customer had probably never seen the competing product but assumed that as it was a little more expensive the quality must be better.

Trade price

The trade price is what you charge stockists to buy from you. The price you set will depend on how much you need to make over and above your cost price in order to cover your other overheads (premises, storage, utilities, etc.) and how much profit you want to make on top of this.

The price that stockists will be willing to pay in relation to the RRP differs depending on the industry and their size.

Setting a trade price

It is necessary to be a little strategic when deciding who to sell your product to and for what price. If it is a high-end, boutique-type product, selling it to eBay sellers is probably not a wise idea, as the sellers will discount it and annoy your bricks-and-mortar stockists.

Thanks to an EU Directive passed in April 2010, as a small-business product creator you have the right to dictate where your product is sold. The Directive states that:

> "The basic principle remains that companies are free to decide how their products are distributed, provided their agreements do not contain price-fixing or other hardcore restrictions, and both manufacturer and distributor do not have more than a 30% market share."[1]

You are also free to charge different prices for different stockists. Having separate prices for online and bricks-and-mortar stockists can be a good way to prevent online discounting. For example, you could choose to charge bricks-and-mortar stockists 10% less than stockists who operate purely online. The different groups of stockists need never know that they are being charged different prices, as trade prices are generally kept quiet.

---

[1] See Commission Regulation (EU) No 330/2010 of 20 April 2010 on the application of Article 101(3) of the Treaty on the Functioning of the European Union to categories of vertical agreements and concerted practices.

I wish that I had known this when I first started selling the Cot Wrap. I was keen to get my product into every shop and on every website I could. After a while, I noticed that the Cot Wrap was selling on eBay for up to £5 less than the RRP. Although my total sales volume was the same, I was getting fewer orders from bricks-and-mortar stockists. Therefore, I made the decision to prevent stockists from selling the Cot Wrap on eBay through our Terms & Conditions of Sale. Luckily, thanks to the EU Directive mentioned above, this is perfectly legal.

Profit margin

The difference between the selling price and cost price of your product is the profit margin, usually given as a percentage. When selling to your stockists, your profit margin is the difference between the trade price and your cost price. When stockists buy your product, their profit margin is the difference between the price they charge the end consumer and your trade price.

Every distributor and retailer will have a target profit margin – they will usually be happy to tell you what this is. Large high street chains have huge overheads – staff wages, rent, heating and lighting for huge stores, and advertising costs – so they will demand much higher margins than small high street stores and online shops.

The easiest way to explain how profit margins work is through a simple example.

Let's say that you can manufacture your product for £1 a unit and in your industry, small, independent shops will require a profit margin of 50%. Your pricing structure will be as follows:

	£
Cost price	1
Trade price for small independent shop	2
End consumer price (excluding VAT)	4

In this simple example, you and your stockist both double the price, making a profit margin of 50%.

Things get more complicated when another party enters the chain. If you are going to sell your product abroad, unless you are willing to set up an office in every country you will have to sell through a distributor.

Also, some major retailers insist that smaller companies go through a distributor. This is because it is easier and cheaper for them to deal with several large distributors who have slick distribution operations, rather than than hundreds of small businesses who will need help in understanding their requirements.

In the following example, the distributor requires a margin of 25%. Assuming you still want the price to the end consumer (before VAT) to be £4, the figures now look as follows:

	£
Cost price	1
Distributor price	1.50
Trade price for major retailer	2
End consumer price (excluding VAT)	4

Your profit margin has now been reduced to 50p per unit (25%).

NB: Both the small independent store and the major retailer would charge VAT to the consumer, so the end price would be £5 (or £4.99 as is commonly charged). As long as you and your distributor/stockists are all VAT registered, none of the other prices would be affected. Registering for VAT is discussed in more detail below.

Margin calculator

In order to help you to work out the margins applicable to your product, I have developed a margin calculator using Excel which you can plug your own figures into – head to **www.productpreneur.co.uk/margincalculator**.

Other issues

Many of the challenges you will face in running a business will be the same as those which any small business will face. As there are plenty of good books which cover these general issues (see the Resources section), I will not cover them in great detail. However, I will briefly cover some special considerations for productpreneurs which differ from those faced by other kinds of businesses.

Company structure

Registering as a limited company will give you a degree of protection if something were to go wrong with the business. As a sole trader, there is no distinction between business money and personal money and all business debts are the personal responsibility of the sole trader.

A limited company, on the other hand, is a separate corporate body that is liable for its own debts. If someone were to sue you for damage caused by your product, as a sole trader you would be at risk of losing everything you personally own. If you had started a limited company, the company would be liable for paying any compensation (although if the damage was very severe, there is a risk that as a Director you could face criminal proceedings).

VAT

With regards to VAT, registering from the outset can be a big advantage for productpreneurs, as you will be able to claim back the

VAT element of the start-up costs that you incur (i.e. your patent attorney fees and the cost of tooling). If you are selling primarily to other retailers rather than directly to consumers, adding on VAT is not a big deal as trade prices are always quoted net (without VAT) and retailers expect to have VAT added on. As almost all retailers will be registered for VAT, they can claim the VAT element of their invoices back.

Also, registering as a limited company and for VAT is a good idea in order to look big. Major retailers will expect their suppliers to be limited companies and to be VAT registered. By not being VAT registered, you are effectively telling everyone that your turnover is less than £79,000 a year (the VAT registration threshold at the time of writing). Being a sole trader screams cottage industry. For more information on whether or not you should register for VAT visit **www.hmrc.gov.uk/vat/start/register**.

Cash flow

When planning a business, most people focus on how much profit they will make. What many fail to realise is that cash flow is one of the most critical components of success for a small business. Without cash, profit is meaningless: it will be invested in the business as stock or as credit to customers and will be unavailable to be paid out to shareholders. More importantly, without enough cash to pay your suppliers, no matter how much profit your business is making, it will fail.

Cash flow management is particularly difficult for productpreneurs who manufacture, as there is likely to be a lag between paying your suppliers (your factory) and receiving the payment from your retail customers. Most overseas factories expect a deposit of 30% at the time of ordering, so they can buy the raw materials, and the remaining 70% at the time of shipping. Shipping usually takes one month, and then after your product is dispatched to retailers, each retailer will expect at least 30 days credit. The cash which you will need to finance this lag (which can be months) is called working capital.

In addition, your retailers will expect you to hold stock at all times so that your product is available to dispatch within a few days. It is usually not possible to manufacture on demand, especially if you manufacture overseas, and you will most likely have to hold stock. The more stock you hold, the more working capital you will need.

Insurance

You will need to have insurance in place to protect your stock, both while it is in transit and while it is in storage. In addition, most large retailers demand that their suppliers have product liability insurance of at least £2m. This will cover you in the event that a customer is injured or has their property damaged as a result of your product.

Safety

Knowing what safety testing you are required to carry out for your invention can be confusing. By law, manufacturers must ensure that their products are safe. As a manufacturer you could be held liable in any legal action for harm caused to consumers or businesses as a result of unintended side-effects or the failure of products manufactured or supplied by you. However, unless your product falls into a high-risk category such as toys, food and electrical items, it can be difficult to identify what legislation or standards a product falls under.

Contact your local Trading Standards office for advice in the first instance. Safety testing companies such as Intertek (**www.intertek.com**) and SGS (**www.sgs.co.uk**) will also be able to advise which tests you should carry out and will be able to do the testing for you. Also, your trade association may be able to help.

Large retailers usually have an in-house quality assurance department and will provide you with a list of tests that you are required to carry out before they will take on your product.

Licensing

When a company licenses your product, they take over the manufacturing and distribution (sales), paying you a royalty per sale. A licensing agreement is usually for a set period of time, e.g. five years. For the duration of the licensing agreement, the licensee will have exclusive rights (either in a specific territory or worldwide) to use any patents and trademarks which cover your product.

Licensing can be a great option if you have a strong patent and don't have the time, money or inclination to set up a business. As the licensee is likely to have more experience and resources than you, they can probably do a better job of selling your product. However, only around 6% of inventors succeed in licensing their product, and the rewards can be very low.

A typical licensing royalty is around 5% of revenue. This means that if the licensee sells your product to a large high street chain at £5 per unit, you will receive 25p per unit sold. If the licensor sells 10,000 units a year (which is considered to be a very good level of sales for the first year of a product), you will make £2,500 a year, less tax. Not enough to retire to the Bahamas unfortunately.

If you were to manufacture your product yourself, let's say that your manufacturing cost per unit is £2. Therefore, selling to a high street chain for £5 a unit will make you £3 per unit. Even after subtracting all of your business overheads, your profit is likely to be much greater than 25p per unit.

How to find a licensee for your product

The big players in your industry may be interested in licensing new products. Do your homework and look for companies that would be a good fit. Before contacting them, make sure you have protected your intellectual property. Otherwise, the companies you approach have no incentive to license your product and pay you a royalty – they might as well just copy it.

Approach potential licensees as you would a major retailer (see Chapter 6). Focus on what your product can do for them rather than what the licensee can do for you. Know your product, industry and target customers inside out and perfect your pitch. Research who the licensee's key people are, what products they sell, their target customers and their distribution channels.

Potential licensees are likely to be very interested in your patent – what areas it covers, which countries you have applied for patent protection in, etc. The stronger your patent is, the more interested they will be in your product.

If the licensee is keen to take on your product, they will provide you with a draft contract which will specify the terms of the licence and the royalties they are prepared to pay (usually negotiable). It is a good idea to have a lawyer look over the contract to make sure it covers everything you want it to.

Inventor Mandy Haberman approached all of the leading companies in the nursery products industry to license her product, the Anyway-Up Cup, an innovative non-spill toddler cup. Although all of the 18 companies which she approached loved her product, none of them ended up licensing it. Mandy believes this is because the industry is very risk-averse, preferring to bring their own versions of successful products to the marketplace rather than developing new products from scratch.

One of the companies whom Mandy visited kept her prototype and, four years later, brought out their own non-spill cup. The company was a large, established brand and Mandy believes that in copying her product, they took a calculated risk – they assumed that as a small player, she wouldn't be able to defend her patent. However, because Mandy's sales plummeted as a result of the infringing product, she decided to risk everything and sue them. Luckily she won – the judge granted an injunction restraining further sales of the infringing cup.

Mandy has successfully stopped a further three large companies from infringing her patent. Her story is fascinating – read more at www.mandyhaberman.com or listen to a 40-minute recording of Mandy's story at **www.shesingenious.org**.

Chapter wrap-up

Finance is generally not a particularly interesting area for productpreneurs but it is crucial to master it in order for your business to be a success. While some productpreneurs will be lucky enough to license their product, the majority will start their own business in order to manufacture, market and sell their product.

I have covered how to raise funds to develop your product, how to set a price and briefly how to manage your cash flow. I have avoided getting into general business topics because areas such as VAT and safety are very specific to whatever type of product you have, but hopefully this chapter has helped to point you in the right direction for further reading (see the Resources section at the end of the book).

CHAPTER 5
Creating a Brand and Spreading the Word

YOU COULD HAVE THE best product in the world, but if no one knows about it they aren't going to buy it. Simple. Although some products sell by word-of-mouth alone, it is usually necessary to push things along by getting your product in front of the right people's noses. Letting people know about your product is done by getting your product into the media – both traditional (newspapers, TV, magazines) and social (Facebook, Twitter, etc.).

People won't buy your product if it is presented shoddily. Your branding and packaging need to reflect the quality of your product. In order to present your product in the best possible way, you need to really understand your customer. People don't buy products, they buy benefits. Look down at the clothes you are wearing right now. Did you buy them simply to keep warm? Or did you buy them because they make you feel a certain way – smart, sophisticated or maybe just cosy?

The process of doing all this is called marketing. It is an all-encompassing term which includes branding, public relations, advertising and social media. Like many subjects I have covered, marketing is a complex skill which people study at university for years. However, assuming that you don't have three years to spare or plenty of cash to pay a professional, it is definitely possible to pick up the basics by yourself.

Branding

If you look up the term 'brand' in the dictionary, the definition you will see will be something like:

> "A type of product manufactured by a particular company under a particular name."

This is the literal definition of a brand, but it doesn't explain why people buy certain brands over others, or why some brands achieve a cult-like following. It doesn't explain why I am writing this book on a Mac instead of a PC with an iPhone and iPad either side of me (I'm a big Apple fan). Or why I will only drink Coca-Cola rather than other brands of coke.

I like Apple products and Coca-Cola because of the way that they make me feel. Using a Mac makes me feel like a cool creative person rather than a dull business person. Buying a can of Coca-Cola gives me one less thing to worry about in my day – I know it will always taste the same. It gives me certainty.

When launching a product, it pays to think very hard about what feeling you are trying to invoke in your customer. Do you want be reliable like Coca-Cola, or trendy like Apple?

The easiest way to do this is to think about your ideal customer. Who are they? What other brands do they buy? What image do you need to have in order to attract them?

Our branding at Safe Dreams, like most companies in our industry, is all about making the customer feel safe. We use the colour blue, which signifies trustworthiness, dependability and security, and white, which invokes the feeling of purity and cleanliness. Very rarely in our industry is the colour black used (it evokes power, drama and sophistication, which is not ideal for baby products). The more design-focused companies use orange (fun, excitement).

Choosing a name

Naming your product and brand is surprisingly difficult. The name needs to be distinctive enough to be trademarked (see Chapter 2) and for the website domain to be available, but it is also useful if it signals to customers what your product does or what your brand is all about.

Safe Dreams used to be called Handro (after my son, Alejandro – pronounced Ali-handro). While the name was certainly distinctive, it gave potential customers absolutely no idea what my product was or what my company did. I later changed the name to Safe Dreams, which reflects our aim perfectly – to give parents extra peace of mind while their baby sleeps.

I have since learned that using your child's name (or a combination of your children's names) is incredibly common amongst parent-run businesses. Sometimes it works, but often it can look very unprofessional and make the business seem like a part-time kitchen table business (not great for customer trust).

The Cot Wrap is a more literal name, as it is explains exactly what the product does (it wraps around the cot and protects the baby from bumps), while being different enough to be eligible for a trademark. However, my first application for a European Trademark was rejected by the Spanish examiner, who felt that the name was too literal. I appealed against the decision by explaining that the term 'cot wrap' is never used in the English language in the descriptive sense, and the examiner luckily granted the trademark in the end.

Web domains

When deciding on a name, you will need to find out if the website address (domain or URL) is available. It is very easy to check, you can search for name availability using any website host (**www.vidahost.com/domains** is highly recommended).

The best domain to get (even in the UK) is a .com. However, .coms are unfortunately the hardest to get, as all the best ones have been bought by savvy resellers who will charge thousands of pounds for them. The second best domain to get is a .co.uk. If possible, get both and any other domain endings. The .org domain is associated with non-profit organisations so is probably not appropriate, while .co is a new domain which has yet to catch on.

Designing your brand

You might think that the most important aspect of bringing a product to market is the quality of your product. But if your product is presented badly – if people Google it and find a hastily thrown up website with images that look like they were taken with an iPhone, a DIY logo and shoddy packaging – they won't trust it.

As a minimum, you need to have a professional-looking logo, business cards, website, packaging and images.

> *"A brilliant business presence is really important to me in that when I first started, the first thing I did was get business cards, because I wanted everybody to take me seriously, rather than just seeing me as a mum working from my kitchen table."*
>
> **Claire Mitchell, Chillipeeps**

Claire is right – if you are selling on Etsy, being a kitchen-table business is acceptable, but if you are selling hundreds of units a week to a major retailer, it is not. You need to give retail buyers confidence that you know what you are doing and you have a team behind you as back-up. Major retailers don't want to deal with a one-man or woman band whose business will fall apart if they get ill and aren't able to fulfil their orders.

Whether you agree with this or not, it is the reality. Your title on your business cards should be 'Managing Director' or 'Creative Director' – choose whatever title you want as long as it makes it seem like you have a whole team of people. Get into the habit of saying "we" when you talk about your business, rather than "I".

Spend as much as you can on your logo, website and packaging before you start to sell your product. Branding design is not an area where you want to skimp. Do not design your own logo (unless you are a professional designer).

Choosing a designer

If you are going to spend a lot of money on branding design, it is very important to do your homework and make sure you find the right designer. I covered what to look for in a product designer in Chapter 3 – the same principles apply to finding a branding designer.

Before speaking with designers, it is best to think about the following:

- **Name and tagline** – Come up with a business name, a product name (make this separate if you plan on introducing more products in the future) and a tagline which sums up what your business/product can offer. At Safe Dreams we have taglines for our products which explain exactly what they are: the tagline for the Cot Wrap is 'The safe alternative to a cot bumper' and for the Safe Dreams brand – which shows what we are all about – 'Safe sleeping for babies, peace of mind for parents'.

- **Your brand values** – Are you going for luxury or mass-market? Do you want to be edgy or safe?

- **Budget** – This is one of the first things which a designer will ask you. They don't ask so they can charge you as much as possible, it is so they can assess whether your project is doable for your budget. Most designers have an hourly rate or day rate. If your budget is £2000, they may spend two weeks on your brand and let you make unlimited changes. If your budget is £200, they may only be willing to spend half a day on the project and designing a logo and website in that time frame is just not possible.

- **Make a list of five brands you like** – This is really helpful for the designer to see. The designer will not copy these brands (if they did it would reflect very badly on them as a designer), but they will use them as inspiration by looking at the colours, the font and the overall impression which the branding creates.

When meeting with potential designers, make sure that the designer understands your vision. It is a good idea to give the designer a written brief which is as clear as you can make it – without this, designers have a tendency to go off on tangents and design what they think you want. Also, make sure you know what you are getting for your money – how much time the designer will spend on the work and how many rounds of changes you can make to stay within budget.

Consistency

Stick with the same fonts and colours on all of your branding material – website, adverts, letterheads, compliment slips, business cards, and even your address labels, if you want to look really professional. Ask your designer for the names of the fonts and the Pantone colour references of all the colours which they used so that you have these for use across your range of material.

At Safe Dreams we use a font called FS Albert which is used by many charities – it is clear, legible and makes our words look trustworthy. It is an expensive font, which is good because it is not overused. There are also many good fonts which are free.

Tip: Save yourself some money on design costs by learning how to use Photoshop. You will then be able to resize images, create simple graphics for your website and even create adverts, web banners and leaflets if you are willing to take the time to learn. This is what Marc Ward, the inventor of Jamm door wedge, did:

"*I probably use Photoshop to 2% of its capacity but it saves me thousands in graphic designer costs so it has paid for itself already. You get better at it and if there is something you don't know, you just go on YouTube and find a tutorial about it. As a small business owner you need to wear many hats to keep the overheads low.*"

Website

Thanks to WordPress (**wordpress.com**), these days building a website is not as expensive as in the past, and you don't need to go to a web programmer every time you want to change something. If you have ever had a WordPress blog, you will already know how easy it is to submit a post, make changes and add widgets (widgets are components and features for your site that offer different features for users, such as an online payment system, or newsletter sign-up box).

I would not recommend building your own website using a template as it will look cheap and the same as hundreds of other websites. Have you ever wanted to buy a product online but been worried about sharing your credit card details with a business you had never heard of? If a business is not willing to invest time and money in creating a well-designed, professional-looking website, it makes customers wonder if they will stick around long enough to send them their products, and deal with any after-sales issues. You therefore may like to draw on the skills of your designer and an experienced web programmer.

Your branding designer will usually create the visual look of your website and then outsource the actual programming to a specialist web programmer. While the design cost will depend on how good and popular the designer is, the programming of a WordPress website (which involves installing and customising a WordPress theme) should only cost a few hundred pounds.

If you are going to sell your product directly from your website, your designer may try to sell you an expensive custom-built shopping cart. There is absolutely no need for this when you are only selling one product – you can get simple WordPress software add-ins (called plugins) that will do this job just fine. You can link this to your PayPal account to allow you to collect the money.

A WordPress shopping cart plugin will cost a couple hundred pounds to purchase and program. I recommend WooCommerce (**www.woothemes.com/woocommerce**). A custom-built shopping cart will cost around £1500 minimum.

Images

Photos

Most potential customers, journalists and buyers will see an image of your product before having the chance to actually touch and feel it. Therefore, your images are incredibly important.

Spend as much as you can on a good photographer, and look for one who has product photography experience. I learned this lesson the hard way when I chose a photographer who specialised in child photography – I ended up with beautiful photos of babies with my product out of focus in the background.

You will need high-resolution cutouts and lifestyle shots. Cutouts are images of your products on a plain white background. Lighting is incredibly important for cutouts, especially if they are white (like my products). Lifestyle shots are images of your product in use.

> **Tip**: Ask for some square images – they are ideal for Facebook. Long images are ideal for Pinterest.

Video

If this book had been written even a year earlier, I would probably have said that it is best to allocate your budget to branding, your website and images, and only invest in a video if there is anything left over (which, let's face it, is unlikely). However, these days, thanks to widely available fast broadband, customers and high street buyers almost expect to see a video of a product in action.

Creating a good video is expensive, especially if there is animation involved, although you may be able to find a media student at your local college willing to help for a reduced price, or – if you are very lucky – for free. If you can't afford it, it is probably best to have no video at all, rather than a poorly-produced one that will reflect badly on your brand.

Packaging

On the store shelves, your product will be competing with thousands of others to grab the customers' attention. It is estimated that customers take approximately ten seconds to decide whether or not to buy a product. Therefore, your packaging has to stand out, catch a customer's eye and explain just why they need to buy it quickly and concisely.

Your product tag line should be able to sum up the benefits that it offers succinctly. It should be displayed boldly, together with some well-written copy containing the selling points of your product. Images are also good for signalling the benefits of a product quickly – you will see in the Cot Wrap packaging (images below) there is a picture of a happy baby in a cot. This is to signal that our products keep babies safe and healthy – a healthy baby is a happy baby.

Packaging also needs to keep your product clean and dry and display it in a way which suits your retailers. For example, most retailers in the UK like to hang soft toys so customers can touch them rather than display them in boxes. To cater to this we created a small hangtag which displays the benefits of our Safebreathe toys, rather than a box, which would make the benefits harder to see.

The images above show the first version of the Cot Wrap packaging, which I created together with my brother, and the second version, which was created by a professional designer. We spent a lot of time on our first attempt and it is really not that bad, but the professional designer's version is much more eye-catching and gets across the product's benefits quickly:

- The plain white background gives the packaging a clean look and makes the copy and images really stand out. To compensate for the lack of colour in the background, brightly coloured stars have been used to make the packaging more attractive.

- The tagline and main benefit of the product are shown in bright fuchsia pink to catch the customer's eye.

- The product benefits (the copy) has been moved to the left of the packaging. Because we read from left to right, our eye will typically fall on the top left of a package first. The designer has also made the key word of each phrase bold to help customers process the benefits more quickly.

- The designer has made clever use of the top-right corner to help customers understand quickly what kind of Cot Wrap to buy for their particular cot. In the original packaging, this gets lost in the page.

Tip: If you are planning on selling abroad, you will save money in the future and increase your chances of finding overseas distributors by translating your copy. Claire Mitchell of Chillipeeps says:

"One of the mistakes I made was not thinking multilingual and designing the first set of packaging in English. You've got to think global these days because of social media. I think it's really important to do that from the beginning with your packaging."

Barcodes

You will have noticed that all products on sale on the high street have standardised barcodes. You will probably have scanned barcodes yourself in the supermarket and the price magically appears on the checkout.

Almost all retailers (with the exception of very small ones who don't have computerised tills or stock systems) will expect you to have a barcode on your product. Many productpreneurs get into a fizz about barcodes, but there is no need.

Yes, they are an extra expense which usually isn't budgeted for, but getting one is simple: all you need to do is join GS1 UK (**www.gs1uk.org**), pay the joining fee of £107 (at the time of writing) and an annual fee of £117, and you can then register as many numbers as you need.

It is also possible to buy single barcodes (a quick Google search will bring up the websites that sell them), which may work out cheaper if you have just one product, but as GS1 is the only official barcode supplier in the UK there is always a risk that an unofficial barcode may one day stop working. If you have thousands of units on store shelves on that day, this would cause you big problems. Consequently, going for a cheap barcode may be a false economy.

The most common system of barcodes used in the UK is EAN. You may also hear the name UPC – this is an older system that is still widely used in the US.

Search engine optimisation

Whatever industry or sector you operate in, an important part of marketing is making your website easy to find on the internet.

Every business dreams of reaching the top of Google for the words or phrases which their customers search for. As 80% of web traffic comes from search engines (80% of which comes from Google) and most people don't look beyond the first page of search results, optimising your website for search engines is a crucial part of building a website.

Search engine optimisation (SEO) is the process of making your website as search-friendly as possible. This is done mainly from using keywords and linkbacks.

- **Keywords** are words or phrases which your customers are searching for. For example, Breffo's potential customers would search for 'iPad stand' and Bananagram's customers 'board games for children'. You need to use these words or phrases as often as possible in the text on your website, without the copy looking unnatural and becoming hard to read.

- **Linkbacks** are links from other websites to yours. The search engine bots place more value on a link the more traffic the website has – for example, a link from the BBC is worth 100 times more than a link from an obscure link directory. The more and better quality linkbacks you have, the higher you will get on the search pages.

You can find out how people are finding your website through an analytics programme – the most widely used is Google analytics (**www.google.com/analytics**). However, I prefer the simpler Clicky (**www.clicky.com**).

AdWords

As building up linkbacks takes time, a good way to kick-start a new website is through AdWords (**adwords.google.co.uk**). Google AdWords are the sponsored links which you see at the top of any Google search and the ads you see at the side of some websites.

You choose a keyword, create a two-line ad and set a daily budget for bidding on your keyword. As AdWords are pay-per-click, it is crucial to ensure that your keywords are correctly targeted.

Advertising

Most small business books will tell you that advertising is a waste of money and it is better to focus on generating PR. However, there are exceptions to this.

An advert in the trade press can be inexpensive (in the baby products industry they begin at around £150) and can be a good way to reach trade buyers. Also, if you advertise with them, trade publications are much more likely to feature your press releases as news stories.

Another exception is advertorials in the niche consumer press. Advertorials are written in the same tone and font as the rest of a publication, and therefore can look exactly like editorial (i.e. content written by the publication's journalists), but are actually written directly by the business. At Safe Dreams we have run advertorials in most of the baby magazines and they have brought in a lot of sales.

Tip: Always include a discount code for your website in any advertising that you do. This gives you a way to assess whether the advert was a success by looking at the number of sales that you get as a result of the advert.

Public relations

Another way to build credibility and get maximum exposure for your product is through public relations (PR): a newspaper article about the story behind your product, a picture of a celebrity wearing or using it, or getting it included in the 'hot' products section of a magazine.

The easiest way to understand PR is to compare it to advertising, as I do in the following table:

Advertising	PR
You pay for space in a publication.	You don't pay for space – you write a press release which sparks the interest of a publication and they feature you for free.
You are in control – you write/design the advert and approve the final version.	The publication is in control – they can use all/some/none of your press release. They may misinterpret some of your words or leave out key parts.
Easy – you decide what you want to say, you receive your invoice and you are guaranteed to be featured in the publication.	Difficult – writing a press release is an art which is hard to master. It is always time-consuming and there is no guarantee that you will get in any publications.
Lacks credibility – consumers are so bombarded with ads, they tend to be sceptical.	Credible – viewed as a third-party endorsement.

A press release is the customary way to send stories and news to journalists. Journalists don't have the time to trawl through hundreds of rambling emails every day. Well-written press releases are straight-to-the-point and easy for them to copy and paste into their publications.

A good press release must be news – it must be new and exciting. For example, a launch for a new, exciting product, or a celebrity who has been spotted using a product.

Should you use a PR professional?

Good PR people are expensive and there is no guarantee that they will be able to generate any coverage for your product. However, they are also masters of the craft of writing press releases and are likely to have good contacts with journalists, which can help them get a story published.

Using a professional to do your PR has one main advantage: as an outsider, they will be able to spot what is newsworthy about your product much better than you can.

Even if you cannot afford to use a PR agency on a monthly contract, if you have no experience of PR it is well worth paying someone to help you to write a press release. There are plenty of freelance PR people around who will do this. You can then do the labour-intensive part – distributing and following-up – yourself.

DIY PR

PR people will tell you that the most important thing in PR is connections. PR agents maintain relationships with the relevant journalists in their field, meeting with them regularly. It is a two-way relationship: the journalists will often call them looking for stories when they are stuck for news and the PR agent will call the journalist when they need to get a client in the press.

However, while this is true to some extent, it is certainly possible to get featured in the press even if you have never met a journalist. I personally managed to get on to the BBC news website and get a mention on the BBC news channel as a result of filling out a contact form at the bottom of a story on their website. I happened to spot the story at the right time – the researchers were looking for a small business affected by the volcanic ash cloud that caused chaos in 2010 – and half an hour later I was interviewed and asked to make a video about my experience!

The best way to approach PR is to try to think like a journalist: what is new and different about your product compared to any others? Why is it interesting? How does it solve a problem that is currently being discussed in the news, or relate to a hot news story? It can be very difficult to step back and think like this about your own product, as you will be used to focusing on minute details rather than the big picture.

If you are good at writing and are able to take a step back and write about your product impartially, it is definitely worth learning how to write a press release.

Writing a press release

Journalists like to receive press releases written in a specific format, which makes them easy to scan over and get the relevant information quickly. You can find a template at: **www.productpreneur.co.uk/pressrelease**.

A press release needs to have a hook – something that will grab the attention of journalists. This is the most important and most difficult part of writing a press release. Below are some ideas for hooks:

New product releases

Both the consumer and trade media outlets for your industry will be very interested in the fact that your product is new. For example, if it is a gadget, there are scores of gadget magazines hungry for news, and new = news.

However, getting featured in the mainstream media can be more difficult as there are hundreds of new products launched each week. In order to be featured, your product has to be something very unique and interesting to the masses. A niche gadget may not interest readers of a national newspaper, unless there is an interesting story behind why it was invented.

Celebrities

As a society, we are obsessed with celebrities. A product worn or used by a respected famous person is almost guaranteed to be a big success sales-wise. It is for this reason that celebrities are sent hundreds of free products by PRs and businesses in the hope that they will be photographed with them, or tweet about them.

If your product is low-cost and something that can be used out of the home (e.g. clothing), it is definitely worth sending 'gifts' to famous people with a personalised note.

Rena Nathanson has used this approach to get glowing testimonials for her board game Bananagrams from celebrities such as Dame Judi Dench and Cindy Crawford.

> *"It's a combination of getting hold of their PR agents and sending them the gift or getting Bananagrams included in 'swag bags' at celebrity events. If the celebrity sends a thank you letter, I ask permission to quote them. Dame Judi sent me a letter thanking us for Bananagrams – it is wonderful!"*

It is now easier than ever to contact celebrities through Twitter. However, the best way to send out a gift is to do as Rena does: send it to their publicist. Many celebrities include the name of their publicist in their Twitter bio, or if not, a quick Google search will usually reveal their details.

Firstly, email or call the publicist to ask if their client would be interested in receiving your gift. If so, let them know that you will send it right away and ask them to look out for it. Follow up a few days later to ask if they have received the gift. Then follow up a few weeks later to ask if their client liked the gift.

Charity

The media love to include feel-good stories of individuals or companies doing a good deed for charity. The bigger the charity and the more you raise, the more likely you are to be featured in the national media.

Awards

Winning a business or product award is not only great for your credibility, it is also a great hook for a press release. Product awards are likely to interest niche and industry media, while business awards will interest local media and, if there is an interesting story behind them, national media.

Forms of media to target

The media channels you can look to target are as follows:

- **TV** – The number one way for your product to reach lots of people is by having it appear on national TV. Patrick Mathews' product the Spiderpodium was featured on *The Apprentice*, in an episode where the contestants had to sell British inventions in France. When the episode was aired, the huge volume of web traffic made both Breffo's own website and the websites of its suppliers crash. Patrick also received phone calls from many of the major retailer buyers who had previously rejected the Spiderpodium.

- **National media** – Newspapers and radio shows like to include human interest stories which will appeal to their readership and sometimes run product features. Cara Sayer, inventor of Snoozeshade, was featured in the *Daily Mail*, the UK's second most widely-read newspaper, in a story titled 'Sleeping on the job: Invention to help babies sleep in buggies could make mummy a millionaire' after being shortlisted for a 'Business Mum of the Year' award.

- **Local media** – It is much easier to be featured in your local newspaper or radio station as filling the pages (or time) with local stories can be a challenge for journalists. The downside is that the audience will be much smaller, and therefore you may only get one or two sales as a result.

- **Trade media** – Being featured in a trade publication is a good way to grab the attention of buyers. Although you are more likely to be featured in the news section if you advertise with the publication, if your story is strong then your chances of getting in are good.

- **Niche media** – Many industries have magazines and websites for consumers who are interested in the latest trends and products. This kind of media love to feature anything new and often need 'experts' for stories – as a product creator in the industry, you are an expert and can pitch for these kinds of stories.

- **Journalist requests** – Every day there are journalists looking for case studies to feature in their stories. Journalists will often post their requests on Twitter using the hashtag **#journorequest** and on forums where they are likely to find case studies. For example, journalists who are looking for mums will post their request on Netmums (**www.netmums.com**). Journalists will also post on Response Source (**www.responsesource.com**), a service which almost every PR company seems to subscribe to. The cost of services like Response Source are prohibitive for small businesses and the volume of requests which you would have to sift through to find relevant ones is too much. However, if you have a friend who works in PR, ask them to forward any relevant requests to you.

Social media

There has never been a better time to launch a new product on a tight budget, thanks to social media. Facebook, Twitter, Google+ and the other social sites make it easy for productpreneurs to reach their customers and encourage them to spread the word.

Many businesses do not understand social media. They will start a Facebook page or a Twitter account, post about their special offers for a week or two and then wonder why no one is following them and give up.

What they fail to understand is that social media marketing is not about selling, it is about building a following. It is a way to start a conversation with your customers – to find out what they think about your products, provide interesting content which they can share with their friends and answer their questions. It is not a quick form of marketing like taking out an ad; social media is time-consuming and there will be a long delay before you see the fruits of your labour.

In order to make the time investment worthwhile, ask yourself why someone would follow you. What value can you provide?

Using Safe Dreams as an example, we ask lots of questions (people love to talk about themselves and their children), we post funny pictures and images of interesting baby's rooms (which we ask for people's opinions on). We also run lots of competitions and always give an extra entry to those who share the competition with their friends.

Every year there are new forms of social media which pop up, and it can be very difficult to keep track of which sites are the best to focus on. The current favourites are as follows:

Facebook

Having a brand Facebook page is a great way to build up a community of fans (or *likers*, as they are now called) who love your brand. To begin with, your fans may consist of your mum and a couple of friends, but if you post some interesting content and encourage your fans to share it with their friends, you will soon build up a good-sized community.

Facebook has been our main form of social media marketing at Safe Dreams. We have over 2600 likers, including 20 to 30 hardcore fans who post regularly. Our Facebook page URL is on our websites, printed on all of our packaging and is at the bottom of every email we send. We also do cross-promotion with other Facebook pages where we will run a competition using one of their products as a prize, offering one of our products in return.

When you are starting out on Facebook, a good tip is to look at what your competitors and peers are posting. A good example is Innocent (**www.facebook.com/innocent.drinks**) – it posts a mixture of humour, interesting facts and quirky stories about its business.

In the past year, it has become much harder for businesses to reach potential customers on Facebook without paying. As a result of being listed on the stock market, Facebook has become much more monetised and has copied Google's model of sponsored links. Every time you post as a business page, you are asked if you want to pay to promote the post, either to your existing likers or to their friends. If you don't, your post will be seen by very few of your likers.

Twitter

As a result of the new costs associated with Facebook, many businesses have begun to focus more on Twitter. The downside is that a Twitter feed moves much faster than a Facebook feed and you are restricted to 140 characters. The challenge is to create snappy tweets which catch people's attention and encourage them to retweet to their followers.

Twitter is great for building relationships with not only potential customers, but also journalists and other businesses in your industry. It is an easy way to approach people who are not very approachable in real life – it is perfectly acceptable to tweet a stranger and start a conversation. If it is a well-known or busy person they may not respond, but you never know.

Pinterest

Pinterest is a virtual pinboard which allows users to 'pin' images which they like or find interesting. Pinned images are automatically shared with the user's followers, who can 'repin' the image and expose it to their own followers.

If your product is visually attractive, Pinterest can be a fantastic form of marketing. You can put a 'Pin' button on every image on your website to encourage people to pin it. When people click on the pinned image, they will come directly on to your website. You can also attract people to your website by writing blog posts on topics relevant to your customers, being sure to include an interesting image and pinning the image on your Pinterest page with a keyword-optimised title.

Instagram

At the time of writing, Instagram is the latest craze in social media. Like Pinterest, Instagram is an image-sharing network but is more focused on users creating images themselves rather than pinning images created by others. It appeals to a younger demographic than Pinterest and, like Twitter, is incredibly fast moving.

Instagram is great for showing images of your product in use and also to give an idea of what goes on in your business behind the scenes. An example of a business using Instagram to great effect is artist Johanna Basford (**www.instagram.com/johannabasford**). Johanna has plenty of shots of her finished work but intersperses these with images of her work-in-progress, the pens she uses to draw with, her studio and even her cute dog. This gives her followers a fascinating glimpse into her daily life and work process.

Chapter wrap-up

Marketing and branding are essential to the success of your product. People need to know that your product exists and your packaging, website and marketing materials need to give them confidence that it is a purchase that they won't regret.

Living in the wireless internet age has made marketing much easier – social media has allowed productpreneurs to speak directly with potential customers and to reach journalists easily. However, in some ways it has increased the burden: even if you are not planning on selling your product through the internet, you are still expected to have a professional-looking website and good online content, including high quality video material.

CHAPTER 6
Getting Your
Product
into Stores

WHILE GOOD MARKETING WILL get your product noticed and spark people's interest, the last and crucial step in the process is closing the sale: convincing the customer to hand over their money or the store buyer to sign off a purchase order.

Some people are naturally good at sales (usually those who are super-confident and bubbly), but most feel a little uncomfortable about selling. The good news is that even if you are not one of the lucky ones born with the gift of the gab, selling is an acquired skill. The more you practice, the better you become at it.

Selling is not something that you should outsource or leave to someone else in the business. You are the one who knows your product best, you are the one who has the most to gain or lose through a sale, so you are most likely the person who can best sell your product.

The ideal way to approach selling is to remind yourself how fantastic your product is and that you are doing people a favour by telling them about it. If it is a potential stockist, you are giving them a business opportunity that could make them money. If it is an end consumer, you are showing them a product that could make their life easier or make them feel good.

Separate yourself from the product – you are simply the salesperson. Don't take knocks personally. If someone doesn't want your product, it is because it is not right for them at this time. Find out why they are not interested, decide if you need to use this information to tweak your product, sales technique or marketing, then move on to the next sale.

Where to sell your product

While some lucky productpreneurs have their product stocked in major stores from launch, this experience is rare. In general, large retailers do not like taking risks on a new, untested product from an inexperienced new business. Consequently, the usual route is to start off selling through your own website, online retailers and small independent stores. Once you have built up a following and created demand for your product, it is much easier to get large retailers to take you seriously.

The avenues through which you can potentially sell your product are as follows:

Through your own website

The UK is the biggest online shopping nation in the developed world, with almost two-thirds of adults using the internet to buy goods or services. Every year we make a greater proportion of our purchases online.

As discussed in Chapter 3, it is quick and easy to get a website built with a simple PayPal button so that people can buy your product. However, it will take time for anyone to find your site, as Google puts well-established websites with lots of traffic and links at the top of the search results. A good way to get around this is by paying for Google Ads (see Chapter 5).

Selling directly to consumers is invaluable for getting feedback on your product, which can help you to improve it and get it ready for major retailers. Although this is the method of selling that will give you the highest profit margin, due to the sheer weight of competition on the internet you are unlikely to get a large volume of sales.

Selling directly is also a good way to find out which marketing methods are best for your product. After sending out an order, you could send your customers a quick survey or form to get their opinion about the product. You can use this feedback to tweak your product, you can put the best testimonials on your website and you can use the information for your press releases and brochures. For example, you could ask customers, "Would you recommend the product to a friend?" and use this information to say, "90% of customers would recommend the product to a friend."

Finding out how people discover your website is a great way to understand which forms of marketing are pulling in the most traffic. You can trace the link or Google search terms through a package, like Google Analytics (see Chapter 5). Or you could have a simple box built into your shopping cart page which asks customers how they found your website.

Tip: Whenever you do any advertising or social media marketing, be sure to include a discount code for customers to use on your website. This means that you can measure the effectiveness of your ad by looking at how many sales you got as a result (i.e. how many customers used the discount code).

Looking at the most popular Google search terms which people use to find your website can help you improve your sales argument. For example, through looking at Safe Dreams analytics I noticed that lots of people were finding our Safebreathe toys through searching for allergy-friendly toys. Although the main feature of the toys is that they are breathable, I realised that there is a gap in the market for allergy-friendly toys. I tweaked the packaging and website copy to emphasise the fact that the toys are allergy-friendly.

Selling through online retailers

Many people are wary about buying products from websites they have never heard of before, especially if there is no phone number or physical address clearly on display (which is surprisingly common). They feel much safer buying products from a website like Amazon where customers can leave reviews about products and sellers. Also, some people can't be bothered to input all of their payment details every time they buy something. With an Amazon account, you can buy products with a single click from your phone.

Marketplace sites like Amazon, eBay and Etsy allow anyone to set up as a seller. However, it is important to choose the right site for your product – eBay is better suited to low-cost, mass market products while Etsy is good for UK handmade craft products. Other sites, such as **Notonthehighstreet.com**, have an application process and charge a membership fee.

> **Tip**: Instead of becoming an Amazon seller, Amazon also operate as a retailer, which means that they buy stock from you. This can be a better option, as they will market your product to the site's millions of registered customers (in return for a marketing rebate – a deduction from your invoices).

When selling online, the quality of your images is very important, as customers are not able to touch and feel your product (see Chapter 5 for tips on getting good images). Reviews and ratings are also crucial as they are regarded as trusted third-party feedback. On eBay, sellers are rated by customers after each sale and as a result sellers will go out of their way to please their customers and service is usually excellent. On Amazon, customers are rewarded for leaving reviews on products with a 'Top Reviewer' badge. Amazon have recently cracked down on 'fake' reviewers – those that are genuine are now marked as 'Amazon Verified Purchase'.

An advantage of selling online is that you can offer customers a wide choice of colours and styles. Amazon have huge warehouses and are happy to stock every variation of a product. In contrast, high street stores have limited shelf space and expensive city-centre stock rooms, so they are more likely to only take one variation.

The big disadvantage of selling online is that the lower overheads of online stores (fewer staff, lower rent, etc.) mean that they can sell products for a lower price (i.e. with a lower profit margin) than bricks-and-mortar retailers. If you are selling to both bricks-and-mortar and online retailers, this can leave you in a difficult position. If customers can buy your product for less than its RRP online, bricks-and-mortar retailers will lose sales and are likely to drop your product from their range.

Independent retailers

Sadly, as a result of competition from online retailers and the supermarkets, small, independently-owned stores are a dying breed. However, there are exceptions – gift shops will always thrive in tourist towns and most people prefer to try on clothes in a store rather than buying them on the internet.

The difficulty in selling to small independent retailers is the sheer volume of them – there are thousands dotted around the country. Many do not have websites and some rarely check their email.

Start with the retailers close to you – the best approach is to send an email introducing your product and asking when would be a good time to drop by. The quickest way to reach large numbers of independent retailers is through exhibiting at a trade show or through coverage in the trade press.

Independent stores are unlikely to be able to order huge quantities, so if you are targeting them you will have to keep your minimum order quantity (MOQ) low. It is also important to bear in mind the cost of invoicing and following up on lots of little orders, both in terms of time and money. A good option to reach independent retailers could be to use a wholesaler or a sales agent (see below).

Distributors

In return for a large chunk of your profit margin, distributors will market and sell your product to retailers on your behalf.

The main advantage of using a distributor is that they will have a large, established customer base and existing relationships with large high street stores. If your product is low-cost and you need to sell a large quantity in order to make a profit, selling through a distributor is probably your best option. However, you will make more money per unit selling to retailers directly. Another disadvantage is if the distributor takes over your marketing, you will lose control of how your product is presented.

Most distributors will want exclusivity. Before agreeing, do your research – look at the other products that the distributor has on their books and talk to the businesses behind them to ask if they are happy with the service they are getting. Meet the distributor (face-to-face if possible) and make sure they understand your product and your target market. Ask them how they plan to market your product and what stores they plan on pitching it to.

Major retailers

The big boys of the retail world. This category now includes supermarkets – in recent years they have grabbed a huge chunk of the market from the high street.

While being stocked by a major retailer is great for building credibility, you have probably read in the media about the ways in which some treat their suppliers. Their massive purchasing power means major retailers are able to change their terms and conditions without any notice to squeeze more rebates from their suppliers or increase their own credit terms. Given the current economic climate, many major retailers have been taking advantage of this power.

Therefore, selling through large retailers may give you a large volume of sales but it is unlikely to make you rich in itself. The greatest benefit is probably the exposure, which is gained by having your product on their shelves.

Major retailers employ buyers, whose job it is to find the most profitable products for the store. Different buyers usually look after different categories of products, and the more experienced buyers are experts in knowing what will sell and what won't.

Reaching buyers can be very difficult – they receive hundreds of emails and calls a week about new products. In the next section I will cover the best ways to grab their attention.

Other sales channels

- **Wholesalers** – A stock *supermarket* for small, independent retailers. The retailers like wholesalers, as they can buy a variety of products and only pay one delivery charge. Also, there will be a minimum order value for the entire order rather than per product, which means that the store is able to buy just one or two units of certain products. Wholesalers will expect a large discount on the trade price of your product, usually around 25%.

- **Sales agents** – Individuals who sell products to a variety of stores, taking a percentage commission of each sale. Sales agents will usually be more interested in high-cost products or businesses who have a large range in order to make enough commission for taking on your brand to be worthwhile.

- **Consumer shows** – Held in large exhibition halls, consumer shows are a great way to talk to your customers face-to-face and get feedback without the expense and commitment of renting a shop. While they can be costly to exhibit at, the idea is to raise awareness of your brand, rather than to make a huge profit on sales.

- **Daily deal sites** – Following the huge success of Groupon, similar sites have now popped up in every industry. Doing a deal can be a good way to raise awareness of your product with people who may never have heard of it. Some sites are geared towards offering their members new innovative products, others are good for a bargain. It is better to do your research to make sure that being on the site won't damage your brand.

- **Drop-shipping** – This is when an online retailer includes your product on their site without physically holding any stock. When one of their customers buys your product, they place an order with you and you post the product direct to their customer. Drop-shipping can be a good way to get on lots of sites in the beginning, but it is important to have a good contract in place to cover what happens if the customer wants to return the item. Also, setting a drop-shipping price can be difficult – the price should be higher than the trade price as you want to encourage retailers to buy in bulk rather than drop-ship.

How to get buyers to stock your product

Making a sale is never easy: retail buyers are bombarded with sales calls and emails and don't have the time to pay attention to everything. Unless you are very lucky and your product is something which really wows a buyer the first time they see it, getting your product on the shelves requires lots of persistence. The process of finding out who the right buyer is, emailing them, sending out samples and following up is hard work.

The main ways in which you can get your product in front of buyers' noses are as follows:

Exhibiting at trade shows

Taking a stand at a relevant industry trade show or fair is by far the best way to put your product in front of large numbers of potential stockists in a short time frame. Hundreds of buyers, big and small, come to one place to actively look for new products to stock. You will have the opportunity to demonstrate your product in the flesh and answer any questions which they may have.

Exhibiting at a show can shave months off the process of getting stocked in a store. Meeting anyone face-to-face is the best way to form a relationship, and buyers are much more likely to remember you if they can put a face to your name.

The downside is the cost – trade shows are very expensive to exhibit at. There is usually a set price per square metre of stand space and you also need to budget for travel, accommodation, printing brochures/flyers and kitting out your stand. A ballpark figure of how much you will spend is £1500 at a minimum.

Trade shows require lots of planning. See Chapter 1 for tips on visiting or exhibiting at trade shows.

A press release or advertising in the trade press

Every industry has trade publications that cover stories and new product launches. A well-written press release may get included in the front news section of the publication (the best option), or you could pay for an advertorial. Advertising in the trade press in general is not nearly as expensive as advertising in the consumer press and can be more cost-effective, as the target audience consists of bulk buyers who can become repeat customers (i.e. stockists of your product), rather than just one-off purchasers.

A good advertorial is written in the same style as editorial (content written by journalists), but is actually written by the advertiser (or their PR representative). Usually an image is included alongside the text, together with an email address, phone number or URL at the end so that potential stockists can get in touch easily.

The downside is that press/advertising is a passive way of reaching buyers – you have to wait for buyers to see your story/advert and contact you. Coverage in the trade press is best if combined with a more active form of finding buyers.

Contacting buyers directly

Sending out emails to prospective buyers is time-consuming but it is the second-best option if you don't have the time or money to exhibit at a trade show.

The biggest challenge can be obtaining buyers' contact details in the first place. Some stores, e.g. Selfridges, publish an email address on their website where businesses can submit details of new products, but most do not.

If you are struggling, the best ways to find buyers' email addresses or phone numbers are as follows:

- **Ask other businesses in your industry** – Unless the business is a direct competitor, usually they will be happy to share a buyer's details.

- Do a **Google search** for phrases such as 'Selfridges Toys Buyer' – you may get lucky.

- Try the **trade press** – Some publications, e.g. Toy News Online, publish a list of major buyers each year. Others may have interviews with buyers in articles on their websites.

- **Search on LinkedIn** – Many buyers have profiles, although they tend to have their job title as 'Buyer at Selfridges' rather than 'Toys and Games Buyer at Selfridges', so for the larger stores it may be impossible to know who is the appropriate buyer for your sector.

Once you have succeeded in obtaining their details, most buyers prefer to be contacted by email initially. The best way to proceed is by sending an email or two and following up with a phone call if you get no response.

When sending an email, make sure that it is personalised to include both the buyer's name and the store name. If a buyer suspects that you have sent out a generic email, they are much more likely to ignore it.

Here is further advice to take into account when drafting emails to buyers:

- **Keep it short and snappy** – Buyers do not have a lot of time to read emails, therefore it is necessary to grab their attention right away.

- Spend time coming up with a **good subject** – The subject line of an email is as important as the title of a press release. It needs to make your email stand out from the hundreds of other emails a buyer will receive each week and intrigue them enough to make them open the email. Making the subject line the name of your product is a common mistake – the buyer has most likely never heard of your product so the title will mean nothing to them.

- **Don't mention prices** – Focus on grabbing the buyer's interest in this first email. Prices can be discussed later if the buyer is interested.

- Include a **small image** – preferably pasted directly into the email.

Rena Nathanson of Bananagrams managed to get into big stores by sending out samples of her board game to buyers:

> "I sent samples with cover letters out to absolutely every single buyer this side of the Mississippi. You have to kind of concede to the fact that you're going to give a lot of stock away and it might sit in somebody's bottom drawer for five years before they look at it. You follow up the following week with a phone call to ask if they received it and you get 'Oh yeah, it's sitting on my desk – I haven't had a chance to play it yet.' You know, that sort of thing."

Tips for pitching to buyers

Be prepared for the moment when you finally get a large buyer to stop at your stand or manage to get through to them on the phone to discuss your product. You may have seen episodes of *The Apprentice* where the teams pitch products to a row of unsmiling high street buyers in dark suits. Obviously this is dramatised for TV, but there are important lessons to be learned from the candidates' mistakes:

Know your product

This is where most *Apprentice* candidates fall down. It goes without saying that you should know your product inside out – what it is made from, who its competitors are, what safety tests it has passed and how long it takes to make.

Do your homework

Before contacting a buyer, visit their store, observe who their customers are and understand their brand.

Who is their typical customer? Why would their customer love your product?

Is your packaging appropriate for their store? Some stores like to display products on shelves, some like to hang things on rails. Large stores may ask you to tweak your packaging to suit their needs, so it is best to be prepared in advance.

Know your financials

On the *Apprentice*, candidates often get their cost price, target price and profit margin confused. Unlike them, you have time beforehand to memorise all of your prices. Be prepared for negotiations – calculate both your target price and the minimum price that you can accept before the pitch. Start with the target price and don't go lower than the minimum price.

Think about exclusivity

Stores love to sell a product or brand which none of their competitors have. They may ask to sell your product exclusively for a period of time, e.g. for the first six months. This is common and if you speak with them very early on, they may even offer to help you to develop the product in return for a period of exclusivity.

Like everything, exclusivity is negotiable. Think carefully before accepting – if it is a huge chain with stores on every high street in the country, you would be crazy not to accept, but if it is a smaller store you may be restricting your distribution unnecessarily.

Don't be intimidated

Be confident during your pitch. Remember that in order to remain fresh and current, stores always need new products. If you have come this far, no doubt your product is a fantastic idea. If a buyer doesn't think so, maybe it is too early for them or not the right fit for their store.

Forget modesty

Be prepared to show buyers how fabulous people think your product is – bring along your press articles, customer testimonials and awards. Show off as much as you can.

Think big

The larger the store is, typically the less they like working with lots of small companies. Some will refuse to work with a small company at all and insist that you deal with them through a distributor.

This is not discrimination against small businesses; it is because it makes their life easier. Dealing with a few large suppliers involves less admin, and if a store is ordering hundreds or thousands of different products a week, they need each product in on a certain day (or hour) and labelled in the right format.

Using a distributor will cut into your margin, so it is always best to encourage a store to work directly with you.

Listen and be flexible

If a buyer has doubts about your product, take them on board and be prepared to change things. Some aspects of your product, e.g. the packaging, can be changed very quickly and easily.

Be prepared

The store will need reassurance that you have the capacity to meet their orders in full and on time. Plan ahead – if your product is handmade by homeworkers, come up with a plan to scale up before your pitch. You don't have to implement it right away – there is usually a time lag before you will actually receive the first purchase order – but you will need to show the buyer that you have thought things through.

Chapter wrap-up

Sales are the lifeblood of any business. Think carefully about which sales channels and retailers are the most suitable for your product. Products that appeal to the masses are great for supermarkets but higher-end, luxury products will be more suited to independent boutiques.

In order to reach buyers, exhibit at a relevant trade show for your industry or spend time putting together a list of buyers to target. Do your homework before the pitch, know your customer (who in this case is a retailer) and remember, from a retail buyer's point of view, big is beautiful.

Conclusion

"The biggest problem most people with great ideas have is just not knowing where to start and what to do. I think that's the biggest barrier to market."

Patrick Mathews, Breffo

BRINGING A PRODUCT TO market is not rocket science; anyone can do it if they are willing to put in the hard work. Hopefully this book has helped to point you in the right direction. Productpreneurs need to be incredibly determined and driven to compete with the thousands of other new products which hit the market each year. In the words of Thomas Edison, "Invention is 1% inspiration and 99% perspiration."

Possibly as a result of being part of the 'X-Factor generation', many people think that coming up with a product idea is a sure-fire way to become a multi-millionaire. They dream of getting a patent on their idea and then licensing it to a big company, retiring to a tropical island and living off the royalties.

The reality is that very few productpreneurs succeed in licensing their products. Licensors are usually only interested in products with very strong patents. Getting a patent is a huge investment for the product creator and, even if they succeed, there is no guarantee that their product will ever be licensed or make any money. Before taking such a risk, you really need to have done your homework and be 99.9% sure that people will buy your product.

Patents are not the be all and end all. There are plenty of successful products on the market that are not patented for one reason or another, but which have managed to remain distinctive from their competitors through unique design or strong branding.

Very few productpreneurs achieve success with their first invention. James Dyson spent five years making prototypes of his vacuum cleaner. In 1983, he launched the first version: the "G-Force" cleaner. Although it was a revolutionary product, which would make life easier for everyone without the need to deal with dirty dust bags, no manufacturer or distributor would touch his product as the loss of dust bag sales would hurt their profits.

Steve Jobs, one of the designers of the most iconic products of our time – the iPod, iPhone and iPad – co-founded Apple at age 21 but was fired at age 30 after a personality clash with a CEO he himself had hired. Jobs returned 11 years later and drove Apple to its greatest successes.

Being a productpreneur is a long-term profession – once you catch the bug it is hard to stop. The more you try, the more you learn and the more likely your next product will be a success.

The most important advice is to take action. Don't just be a dreamer. Develop your idea. Find out what others think of it. Protect it. Find out how much it will cost to produce. Research manufacturers. Do anything – just start.

Further Resources

Patents

The Intellectual Property Office (**www.ipo.gov.uk**) has some very helpful resources to help you write the first draft of your patent:

- 'Patents: Essential Reading' (**www.ipo.gov.uk/p-essentialreading.pdf**) covers the basics of patents.

- 'Patents: Application Guide' (**www.ipo.gov.uk/p-apply.pdf**) is a very thorough step-by-step guide which will guide you through the whole process.

- *The Patent Writer* by Bob DeMatteis was written for US patents but it is still good reading for the UK.

Design rights

The Designer – Manufacturer Innovation Support Centre (**www.fashion-manufacturing.com**) has the following excellent guides, which are intended for fashion designers but are applicable to all kinds of products:

- Design rights:
  www.fashion-manufacturing.com/wp-content/uploads/2012/04/CFE-IP-DesignRights-Download.pdf

- Trademarks:
  www.fashion-manufacturing.com/wp-content/uploads/2012/04/CFE-IP-Trademarks-Download.pdf

- Copyright:
  www.fashion-manufacturing.com/wp-content/uploads/2012/04/CFE-IP-Copyright-Download.pdf

- Licensing:
  www.fashion-manufacturing.com/wp-content/uploads/2012/04/CFE-IP-Licensing-Download.pdf

Business basics

- **Gov.uk** (formerly known as Business Link) and Business Scotland (**www.business.scotland.gov.uk**) have comprehensive information covering all aspects of starting a business.

- HM Revenue & Customs (**www.hmrc.gov.uk**) covers everything to do with tax.

Marketing

- *Build a Brand in 30 Days: With Simon Middleton, the Brand Strategy Guru* by Simon Middleton

- *Marketing to Win: How Small Businesses Can Do More With Less* by Jacqueline Biggs

Selling

- *Pitching Products For Small Business: How to successfully prepare your business, brand and products, and sell to retail buyers* by Laura Rigney

- *How to Sell to Retail: The Secrets of Getting Your Product to Market* by Clare Rayner

Other resources

- Productpreneur website: includes a margin calculator, a sample non-disclosure agreement (NDA), sample press release and lots more resources:
  www.productpreneur.co.uk

- UK Business Forums: a very busy forum where you can ask a question on any aspect of starting a business and be sure to get a quick answer:
  www.ukbusinessforums.co.uk

- She's Ingenious: a members-only website for female inventors, including fantastic interviews with successful inventors and experts:

www.shesingenious.org